# THE DIVINE ENCOUNTER

# THE DIVINE ENCOUNTER

## MY REAL LIFE SPIRITUAL EXPERIENCE
## OF MEETING THE SUPERNATURAL

### STEVEN TAGA MAPEPA

Print information available on the last page.

Rev. date: 04/15/2016

**To order additional copies of this book, contact:**
Xlibris
1-888-795-4274
www.Xlibris.com
Orders@Xlibris.com
738673

# ACKNOWLEGEMENTS

My most profound gratitude goes to the triune God- the trinity-God-the Father, the Son, and the Holy Ghost for an extraordinary spiritual encounter. I truly give my deepest heartfelt thanks to Him for the rescue from death, and ultimately giving me a supernatural spiritual experience. This extraordinary sacred experience, consequently, gave me a Divine Encounter.

I also wish to extend my sincere thanks to the wonderful team of the first responders comprising of the Police force, the Fire Fighters, and the Paramedics for their unequalled professionalism in the timely manner in which they handled my near tragedy and impending demise. They arrived at the scene of the car accident promptly, and in a prudent manner in a matter of split seconds made the necessary difficulty decisions and discharged their actions in a highly professional manner by the way they performed their work and successfully recuing us from the car- wreck.

Sincere thanks also go to my senior Pastor Papa Joshua Florian Kamanda, also serving as Chaplain at Indiana University Methodist Hospital and trauma center, the founder, visionary and leader of the Restoration International Christian Center for foregoing and putting off his clocking off time from the trauma center Hospital to come and join the medical team and play his spiritual role to encourage and pray for me, my wife Brenda Sombo Mutwale Mapepa, and our youngest daughter Rudo as we received medical attention and underwent surgery.

And indeed, thanks to the expertise of the entire Hospital staff that attended to us. This includes the Doctors, Surgeons, Nurses, Assistants and their support at the Indiana Methodist Trauma Center Hospital for expeditiously making accurate evaluations, examinations, deciding and executing their action plans to conduct surgeries right on time at the Emergency Center floor. This medical team saved our lives and made sure we were safe and out of danger.

And also our heartfelt thanks to Pastor Steven Cooper and his wife Josie for being there in good time to come and visit us. Special thanks and recognition go to my own brother, Senior Pastor, and overseer for the mid-west region for Forward In Faith Ministries International, Dr. Caleb Mashushire for not delaying to come and visit us at the Hospital and consequently making several follow up visits to come and see us and provide all the necessary help in various ways. He also validated, confirmed, supported, approved of my story's credibility, and substantiated my supernatural spiritual experience, which, for many, was hard to believe. I am also indebted to my most wonderful friend, Martin Landwerlen. You are one of the nicest and most gentle human beings I have ever known. What a wonderful joy of hearing you agree and share your own out of body experience, and let alone working with you as Music Director at RICC. The coffee and cookies you bought and brought me were so nice. I really enjoyed eating them. You are a great and talented Musician, humble soul and wise leader.

Great thanks to Ivy Choga and Nettiwe Mushangwe Bwalanda for being there to cheer me up when I was just taking my first 'baby-walking-steps' as I was starting to learn to walk again after the traumatic injuries I had suffered and was still enduring. You sang for me cradle songs with joy and took memorable pictures I still keep as seen in this book. What an unforgettably incredible moment! Very encouraging! Thanks to my sister Mercy Mudzonga for making it in very good time, it had a good healing effect, God bless you.

Very, very special recognition and greater thanks go to my mother-in-Law, Mrs. Mc Bee, Bertha Mutwale for putting away everything else aside and travelling all the way from Chicago Illinois to come and see us her children. Indeed great thanks to her for going above and beyond the call of duty to decide to stay and lose her work days to stay with us at our home taking care of us and the kids- her grand children- Rungano, Rutendo and Rudo. What a significant support. We could never ask for a better mother. You are the only one we have in the United States of America as we are so far away from home, Zambia- Africa. Indeed, you played your special role as a Mother would do. God bless you more abundantly.

Thanks to Dr. and Mrs. Mizinga, uncle Handa and Grace Siangonya and their last born girl child Luwi, Dr. Mhandi Chinyadza, Tiffany my nurse, my friend and "younger brother, my Timothy" Lester David Scott, your love, care and compassion and tears are second to none. My co- worker in the Lord Mr. Elois Muzondo, many blessings be upon you! Your silent presence, quiet and humble countenance and your usually unspoken love and encouragement speak volumes even your silence that speaks louder than your words of comfort. Thanks indeed to Sabrina Ellen Borden Curtis and her daughter Breyauna for showing so much love by coming to the Hospital to see us during that very critical and fragile stage of our healing process. May God greatly bless you for your love, care, and true act of kindness and compassion. Our hearts also go to aunt Edith Kumwenda for her always remaining a member of our family and a 'grandmother' to our kids. God bless you abundantly. Our hearts go to sissy Tarirai Shiri for the amazing love and visit with food to nourish our broken bodies. God bless you indeed.

On behalf of my wife, Brenda Sombo Mutwale Mapepa and children, I would like to say we are so humbled, honored and overwhelmed by an incredible outpouring of love, support, compassion, well wishes and help in all areas, not limited to material, physical, social, spiritual and financial, but beyond and above to all, but more especially at this point, our hearts go to

Pastor Marvelous and her husband Owen Ndhlovu who juggled with unbelievable acts of sacrifice by doing so much in making sure our kids were taken good care of and took them to school every single day and never missed class attendance. They took our kids to school all the way from the west side of Indianapolis to another school district on the far South side of town in Greenwood at Southport Elementary School. Suffices to also thank the Principal of Southport Elementary School, Mr. Daniel Mendez and his Vice Mrs. Laura Hansell who went out of their way and usual duties to call on us and just check on how we were doing and giving us words of comfort and encouragement. We greatly appreciate your love, care, concern, and friendship.

Thanks to the Zambian community individuals the likes of Mr. Henry Ndhlovu and Yvonne Malukutila, Gladys and her just newly arrived sister from Zambia for coming to the Hospital to see us, great Thanks to Mama Dee Rachael and her kids from the RICC Daycare. Thanks for the food, and financial gift. Great support. Much love go to Mama Overseer, Pastor Tina, Dr. Mashushire (again) their son Caleb, (C J) for the recognition of serving the LORD together for nine years in Forward In Faith Ministries International, in Indiana, Indianapolis. Indeed, thanks to Mr. Jackson Jackson for the hospital visits and providing transport to my first review to Doctor's appointment.

More thanks to pastor Willie Peters and his wife for coming over to our house to pray with and for us. Mamie, thanks to you for coming to visit us at that very critical time of our initial healing process after our early Hospital discharge. You actually came on a much later visit and reminded me how I couldn't even talk the first time you came. To you Alex Maasa and your wife Robina; thanks for the timely visit and prayers, material and financial support. We extend our very special thanks to Vusi for coming over to visit us. We cannot thank you enough for going an extra mile to giving our little Dodo a bath, let alone what happened to you a little later after our tragedy; may God comfort, strengthen and give you divine direction, guidance and wisdom for the rest of your journey in this life. Mr. and Mrs. Mthetwa, thank you for the visit, love and friendship over the years.

The list is too long and due to memory limitations, please do accept my apologies if your name is not mentioned or does not appear here on the list, please do bear with me, it's not on purpose, may the Almighty God richly reward you for all the good acts of kindness and generosity you extended to me and my family in those tough times. It was hard, but with your love and support you made our hard road easy to travel. May God richly bless you all.

# PREFACE

The sole purpose and objective of this story in this book is to share an extraordinary testimony of the mighty divine and sacred power of God. I'm telling you of His mercy and grace. I give all glory to Him, and Him alone; for He alone deserves the glory and honor which is due to Him. God made it clear in His word that He does not share His glory with anyone else. This story intends to do nothing else but to declare the absolute truth of His word and goodness

My wife and I would like to thank Him for His compassion and grace which are more than sufficient for us. As I write every single word and line in this book, I'm reminded that we all must remember that our God says He's a jealousy God who will never share His glory with anyone. He is an eternally loving and caring Father. The psalms of David declare that our God is a strong tower, our place of refuge, our cave and rock upon which we stand in times of trouble and need. His wisdom, knowledge, understanding and divine providence are equal to none. He deserves all the praise, honor, and worship from all His creation.

This story and account is intended and directed at exalting Him and lifting His name as our most high God. He is much higher than any other name here and far beyond our minds can fathom or comprehend. There is no other name higher than the name of the LORD, our creator and ancient King of the universe. He is the greatest of all beings known and unknown, knowable and unknowable. He is all knowing, all present and all powerful. He is truly the King of kings and LORD of lords. He is the mystery and desire of ages. He is ever-living, ever-loving, and ever-lasting. He's all good, perfect and holy. He's all kind, all loving with immeasurable grace for His children. We are His treasure, and the crown of His creation.

This story is an account about a tragedy, but the provident power, wisdom, and loving kindness of our creator rescued us from the cruel cold hand of death. Therefore, it's not the rescued that should be perceived as heroes, but it is the rescuer who is the sole hero. My wife, daughter and I were rescued from all afflictions that included death itself which was defeated some two thousand years ago on the cross where Jesus Christ our Messiah, Emmanuel- the God who is always with us who, even though we walk through the shadow of the valley of death we fear no evil for He is with us, as written in Psalm 23:4. The end of our end became the beginning of our beginning. Instead of dying, God gave us another chance to live, for which we're forever grateful for His undeserved and unmerited favor upon our lives.

# CHAPTER ONE

I find it unusual, and indeed an amazing paradox that I do not experience, embrace or express mixed emotions as I retell this tragic story. Instead of experiencing and expressing sadness, I tell this story with a feeling of an attitude of immense gratitude in my heart, soul, mind, spirit and being. This incident and accident occurred on the 9th of September, 2015. Instead of telling this account as an extraordinary story, I tell this event as an ordinary story.

The epicenter or centerpiece of this story is to give God all the glory. My heart is full of thanksgiving to God for His unmerited favor; His immeasurably abounding grace for my family- my wife, little daughter and myself. The three of us got involved in a terribly breathtaking car-crush. This was a car accident of unimaginable magnitude by all accounts. Had it not been for God's mighty hand that strongly descended upon us and rescued us, we'd have perished and counted among the dead. We'd have been recorded in the books of history. Our God came to the rescue by way of divine intervention.

The car accident was a shaking, a shifting, and a lifting of our lives in the intensity and level of our faith in God, our love for Him, divine connectivity to His sacred and divine being and infusing us in His very divine being. It all turned out to becoming a divine encounter. It became a sacred experience and medal of unexpected honor in our faith levels and spiritual dimensions of our destinies. Our destinies and directions of life suddenly took a radical change. An immediate lifting and transformation took place due to this strange occurrence.

This is a story that was birthed out of a terrible tragedy. This kind of a tragedy is not a thing I'd wish for anybody, let alone my wife, daughter and indeed myself who found ourselves in this car accident. The accident moved from being just an ordinary incident to an extraordinary life event. It changed from a natural to a supernatural one, from a physical to a spiritual experience, and from a human occurrence to a divine encounter. Indeed, a radical spiritual revolution.

I want to tell the account of this story with all the sincerity, accuracy, and humility which only God can provide. On this particular day, 09-09-15, I woke up as on any other ordinary day. As I got up and started off driving for work in the early hours of this pre-fall morning. Just as I was turning off Thompson road 465 ramp onto the US 31 going on to connecting to the 465 West highway to Georgetown in the State of Indiana, in the City of Indianapolis in the USA. Something very strange somewhere in the atmosphere was in the air and was about to happen. Something very strange would happen to me on this particular day.

As I pulled up close to a vehicle ahead of me, a premonition kicked in and triggered a thought of caution that flashed through my mind, to not get so close to a vehicle in front of me in order to avoid the possibility of a potential accident; just in case the other driver decides to back up and would directly hit my Chrysler, LHS of 1999 model. This kind of car was a very solid and heavy car made of metal with unequalled balance only matched to a Mercedes Benz car. That was a kind of strange thought that had crossed my mind.

It had been a very long time since I had been involved in an accident. For some time now, my wife had commended me for good driving. She said I was exercising caution and alertness in my driving. I was confidently proud of my driving record and experience. Admittedly, I had got involved in some minor accidents before this one I'm writing about. These past minor accidents never turned out fatal and had negligible consequences at most.

As a transport coordinator for my church – Restoration International Christian Center Daycare ministry, where I did my pick- ups and drop-offs of the Daycare kids at their respective schools. Strangely, one thought had been playing through my mind over and over that morning. The thought in question was in the nature of what I have come to dub as:" My divine Inspirations" which I usually shared on my Facebook Timeline "What is on your mind" to which my Facebook friends respond with likes and comments. The thought went like this: "From what may seemingly look good, something bad can be birthed out of it, and from what may seemingly look bad, something good can be birthed out of it." This is not only a contradictory idea but a classical example of a paradox. It is seemingly self-contradictory.

As I was winding down the day, I decided to pick- up my little one and half year old daughter from our RICC Daycare so that I could also pick up her Mom, my wife at a business premises called J.J Treasure strove Furniture shop and drop them off at home so that I could return back to church for a leadership meeting. During these meetings, our senior pastor, Joshua Florian Kamanda took time to teach, train, and coach, us on leadership skills. As I am writing this book, I'm serving on the Church Pastoral Board as Assistant pastor and Ministry coordinator for RICC under Senior Pastor Kamanda's leadership as Founder, and Visionary. On this particular evening I was going to watch a video on "Leadership Levels" by the legendary teacher on leadership John Maxwell with my co-Assistant Pastor for Administration, Marvelous Bunu Ndhlovu

In fact, as I was about to leave the church and Daycare premises with my youngest daughter Rudo, Pastor Marvelous had come up to me to ask why I was going all the way to the south side of town when the leadership meeting was so up close. She came up to me and said, "Pastor Taga, where are you going?"

I am taking Dodo (as I fondly call my youngest daughter with her nick-name) home so she does not have to stay late."

"Ah! Pastor Taga, why?" she looked at me as a way to suggest that I should not go. She lowered her eyes with a look of disapproval of my idea to go.

However, I got into my car and buckled Dodo in her car-seat and drove away towards the South. Did I ignore, disregard, or override her advice or suggestion? I think, in all honesty, yes, I did. May be, so that the inevitable would happen?

As I approached exit 2B off the ramp running into US31 street we reached past a suburban shopping center along Thompson road; I heard my little daughter call out, shouting: "Mommy! Mommy! Because it looked similar to the buildings around the place where her Mom worked at the Hair- braiding Salon and sewing shop where she was waiting for us. We arrived and picked her up and got into Madison Avenue headed south.

We were certainly having a good end of day chat. My wife was updating me on current issues she thought I should know about. This took us up to Stop 10 which is a four- way intersection street. As we were approaching the intersection, the traffic lights turned green. As a cautious driver, I went ahead to check on the oncoming traffic from the opposite direction, in order to make sure we were safe and cleared to turn left. Just in front of me was a truck that was waiting for a turn to go right. It was getting ready to turn on the opposite direction turning lane, I made a cautious judgment that the way was clear for me to turn. I proceeded with all the caution I could master.

No sooner had I started turning left did I see a small blue car in terrific high speed coming from the opposite direction. Instinctively, I had to make a very quick decision in the wink of an eye. According to the principles of Psychology, when one is faced with danger, there are two options available, either to fight or flee; So, I quickly made a decision to step hard on the gas pedal and speed off in order to flee from the imminent danger. Little did I know that the decision to speed off did nothing to change the inevitable impending potential dangerous situation. Within a flash of second, something tragic had already happened so suddenly just like I'd been hit by flying bullet. I'd just heard a sharp piercing sound. It wasn't a loud bang, but a soft sound like an object in great speed passing by. That was it!

In the following moments, I came to realize that I had just got involved in a terrible car accident. Directly in front of me was the dash board that I was looking at. What I saw shocked me. There were a lot of internal wirings that had popped out and the car was totally mangled with a lot of internal stuff sticking out all around the car.

At this point I looked back at my wife and daughter who were my passengers sitting at the back. To my great surprise and shock, I observed that my wife had instantly developed a big bulging bump on her forehead, and my daughter was hysterically crying on top of her lungs. Indeed, it dawned to me that the unexpected had happened. A greater tragedy than I'd expected. All of a sudden, I discovered I was locked in a car-wreck beyond description. I was torn between accepting that this was reality, a dream or just a nightmare I could quickly wake up from. It was clear to me that I had just been badly struck by another car, so hard and so bad. I was inside of a car- wreck hard pressed from both sides- left and right.

I was in this an unbelievable car- wreckage of unimaginable magnitude. Total destruction had been done to our car in a flash of a second. And oh LORD! the bulging bump on my wife's forehead was part of the evidence of how terrible the accident had an effect on us. It was instantaneously recorded on mind that out of all the minor car accidents I've had in the past were by far not compared to this particular one. This particular one was not only terrible and major, but the worst of them all in all my driving history and record. As I took a third look at my wife's bulging bump on her forehead, I heard her say: "Honey, let's go home, the kids are all by themselves." She was referring to our ten year old, fifth grader; and our first born child, our son Rungano and eight year old, third grader, second born daughter, Rutendo.

In fact, we were just a few hundreds of yards away from joining them at our apartment home at Windsor Court. They'd just returned from Southport Elementary School where they both attended school, and were waiting for us to return home from work.

The exact time of the accident was 5: 54pm according to Police report records. Going back to what my wife had said to me; in response, I just looked at her in surprise and shock at how she could not grasp the magnitude of the terrible nature of the accident we'd just got involved in and how she could not feel the hurt on her forehead and also how she couldn't see the extensive damage that had been done to our car. Our car had sustained an instant "mechanical-paralysis" so much so that the car could not even move an inch or, let alone, even drive any more. My wife's suggestion for us to go home and join our kids would have not been lawful even if the car would have been able to drive. According to the law, we're not supposed to move away from the scene of the accident. It's illegal and a violation of traffic laws and regulations all around the United States of America and other countries. The rule demands that you wait at the scene of the accident until the Police come and make a thorough assessment and investigation of the nature of the accident and determine the probable cause and decide what went wrong and write and produce a Police report.

The other thing that was not only troubling and deeply concerning that shook me to the core of my very being, was the questions that my wife asked me in the midst of all this clearly evident confusion and tragedy; she asked me the following two questions and said: "Honey, where're we?" "What has happened?" It suddenly truck me that she was not only disoriented and shocked by the impact of the accident, but definitely confused, because she didn't know where we were and did not know what had just happened to us.

At this point, I decided to attempt to move my own body in an effort to get out of the car so that I could assess the nature of the accident and evaluate the extent of the damage that had been done to our car. It was during this effort that, as I tried to move, I felt a total disconnect running from my shoulder going down through to my rib-cage up to my waist. As if that was not enough, I actually heard a sound of broken bones making splattering sounds splashing in my body-fluids inside, around and under my rib-cage. To my shock and surprise I felt a sharp pain running from my neck all the way down to my waist. I realized that I had sustained serious internal injuries. I knew without any shadow of a doubt that I had suffered broken bones because of the splattering and splashing sound I was hearing. My broken bones were basically splashing in a liquid right inside of me. This realization was traumatic!

It was not only the sharp pain, but an extremely excruciating kind of pain rendering me totally immobile. I turned to wife and said to her, as if talking to myself; I said: "Surely, honey, how could I come all the way from home in Africa, and to such a far off land, only to come and die here?" My wife answered me back and said:

"Honey, don't talk like that!"

I immediately understood that she didn't have the slightest idea of what I meant, and let alone, what grave internal injuries I knew I had sustained. I understood that she was right because there was no visible sign to show scratches, bumps, and bruises, and nothing for her to see the invisible internal injuries that only I could feel inside. There was no external wound or cut on my body, and indeed, no sign or flow of blood visible to the naked eye. Because of this I fully understood why she couldn't know or understand what I was talking about. But in any case, as the old saying goes: "Who feels it, knows it." But in the real sense, I was badly hurt and bleeding inside.

The truth is; not even I, myself had the slightest clue as to what extent or degree I had been injured. As if all this was not enough, I began to feel the very breath of life leaving me and fading away. I was acutely and quickly running out of breath. I was experiencing an acute shortness of breath. My breath had suddenly become shallow and was no longer deep enough as would be considered normal inspiration and expiration in human respiration according to biological terms of normal inhalation and exhalation. My respiratory system was evidently messed up. There was no doubt left in mind, at this point, I was convinced that I had began experiencing the most dreaded process of dying. That was not only a scary thought but a hard reality to accept and a bitter pill for me to swallow. Questions about how my young children would remain alone without a father and or without a mother because I had no idea how this ordeal would end. I was equally concerned about my father, brothers and sisters and all my relatives back home in Africa; even the more critical concern of them all, if my wife would die; I began to feel a lot of guilt and self pity in the face of all these scenarios likely to unfold. I was in dire straits and a critical quagmire. I vividly saw all my dreams, aspirations, purpose of life, God's promises to me and my destiny tumbling, crashing and crumbling right in front of my face because I had began to feel the grip of death encroaching on me. What a tragedy to me and all connected to me. You can just imagine the barrage of the train of thoughts that bombarded me and were running through my mind.

As this reality was evidently unfolding, I knew it was time to make some tough urgent decisions. These decisions had to be made quickly because time was of the greatest essence and was not on my side. I needed to do this before my breathing could cease. I would breathe my last breath at any time now.

Fortunately, my mind was very sound and alert. I was fully aware of the realities surrounding me and the challenges that required my quick decisions before my impending demise would materialize. I was quick to know and understand what I had just been involved in. I knew exactly what was going on and was most likely to happen to me in the following moments that were quickly ticking away and fast approaching. So, I hurriedly reached for my phone. Sadly, my ear-piece or blue-tooth was gone and nowhere to be found as I frantically tried to find it in order to make some important calls in the few critical moments left before I could lose my breath.

Thank God, My phone was still able to send a call without it, which, in normal circumstances was unusual and most unlikely to be easy to do. I checked on the most recent calls I'd made in the course of the day, and there it was, right on top was the phone number I needed to make. I hastened to dial and managed to call and reach Pastor Marvelous Bunu Ndhlovu, my co- Assistant Pastor for administration who was the last person I had talked to before my departure from the Church and Daycare premises. This was God's providence to have her number on top of the list of previous calls I'd made. I was able to make a quick call to her. As soon as I pressed on her number even before I could hear the buzz, she picked up.

With a soft, low, and calm voice I began to speak, I could not speak with a loud strong voice due to the pace at which I was losing my breath which had greatly decreased by now. In the usual manner I address her, I said:

"Mama, could you please go to my house and get my children, Rungano and Rutendo (my son and daughter) who are all by themselves because I won't be able to go home now because I've just got involved in a serious car accident." In response, she just replied without any question and said:

"Yes, Pastor, I will."

I'm sure she quickly understood because of the way my voice was sounding. It wasn't my usual tone of voice. There was something unusual in it. It was sad, somber and solemn with traces of shock and despair. I also mentioned that:

"Could you please go there quickly before the Child Protective Services could discover that the children are all alone? I really don't know what will happen to me from here any time from now."

# CHAPTER TWO

All of a sudden we were bombarded by an influx of the arrival of the First responders that comprise of, the Police, and their Police cars, the Fire Fighters and their Fire-trucks, the Paramedics, and their ambulances and the towing truck along with them.

The air was filled with loud sounds of sirens from the Police cars, Fire-trucks, and ambulances. All of them were blustering through the evening air and sounded like an orchestra of the music of sirens with different but combined tone colors. The timbre or different tone colors of siren sounds produced a kind of home- going sacred harmony with a very unusual polyphonic texture. All these various sounds were signifying danger as they all surrounded the accident scene.

The several flashing lights from them all had various colors of red, blue, and silver flashing all around us. I saw that we were surrounded by men in uniform, each looking different, belonging to their respective different departments of Police, fire, and ununiformed Paramedics.

Earlier on, before their arrival, I'd seen a tall lean woman with a cell phone stuck on her ear talking and walking around a damaged car. I was definitely sure she was surveying, inspecting, and assessing, the damage that had been done to her own car. I am sure this was the woman who had just T-boned me. Due to the speed at which she was travelling, she'd pushed my car into another oncoming vehicle on my immediate left. This other car is the one that had crushed the door on my side and caused me the serious injuries I had sustained. The car that had hit me from the right had definitely come with so much momentum and force that it was able to push such a heavy car like my Chrysler LHS. My Chrysler had so much weight and balance only equal to a German made Mercedes Benz. She'd hit directly at the door where my wife and daughter were sitting on the rear seats of our car.

On this particular day, for some unknown reason, my wife had decided to sit at the back of the car so that she could play with her little daughter whom she'd not seen and missed for the whole of that fateful day because she'd been at the Daycare. In the midst of all these noises and flashing lights all around us, our daughter, Dodo (so fondly called) was wailing and crying hysterically on top of her shrill voice. While on the other hand, to my greater shock, the bulging bump on my wife's forehead had worsened and my mind was still racing through the questions she'd just asked me confirming disorientation and confusion due to the impact. I was deeply saddened by the way the events were unfolding and turning out.

Moreover, to my greater surprise, as she later told me, she was not aware of all that was happening around us. She didn't see what was taking place. In spite of all the loud sounds and the noise that the sirens were making, she heard nothing. She didn't see the flashing lights all around us and did not even see the First Responders who were frantically trying to make way into our wrecked and mangled car. She'd passed out already.

The specific men in uniform I saw who appeared on the scene were the Fire-Fighters. They stood in front of us and started advancing towards our car after they had made a quick assessment of the damage that had been done to our car. After examining our car, they held a brief consultative meeting among themselves. After talking among themselves, they seemed to have settled on a strategy to rescue us. They had agreed on an emergency rescue plan and the strategy was to have quick access to us as we were the trapped occupants in the mangled wreck.

Without hesitation or any further wasting of time, I saw them throw a tent like material to cover us as they began to break the car's windshield using their equipment and machinery. They started chiseling and cutting away the windshield and left door of the car which is the side where I was. They swung into action with lightening speed and gained access into the car wreck and began to whisk us out one at a time. In as much as my memory could recollect and serve me well, I cannot still remember seeing how they fished out and whisked both my wife and daughter away into the ambulance and drove them away to the Hospital at which point my wife had already passed out and was unconscious as she came to tell me much later during our recollections and reflections.

I can only remember finding myself in the hands of two fire men laying me down on a stretcher stretched out and waiting for me. As they carried me over onto the stretcher, the pain in my body augmented to such an increased level and a degree so high that I could hardly bear it at that stage. The handling and movements of my body by the Fire Fighters worsened the pain with so much acute sharpness around my chest area, the zone that had suffered grave injuries. I mourned and groaned and even tried to scream, yell, and shout due to the intensity of how I was hurting inside. Within a very short time I found myself inside the Ambulance. Inside the Ambulance was a Paramedic who also quickly swung into action and began to exam the places, parts, and extent of the injuries I had sustained. He asked where in my body I was feeling more acute pain. He wanted to identify my body parts and positions with prevalent sharpness of pain. The body part with the most prevalent pain was my chest area, specifically, around my rib-cage. Both the right and left sides of my rib-cage, coupled with sharp pain on my shoulder and the lower head region on the left side of my neck.

I went on to tell him that I was also experiencing a continuous process of acute shortness of breath. At this point I was almost failing to inhale and exhale. My respiratory system was quickly failing and almost coming to a gradual halt. I was deteriorating at a gradual but fast rate. Looking at the pace things were going, I was going to expire and die at any time as moments were quickly passing by.

Just as we were getting ready to go before the Ambulance could take off I saw a Police Officer jump into the Ambulance, and hovering and towering over me as I was laid helplessly on the stretcher where I'd been placed just minutes ago. In a low, soft, but audible voice "What's your name?" he asked me, I sheepishly answered him and said,

"Steven Taga Mapepa." Inclining his ear towards my lips as if to let me know he'd not understood me, he asked again:

"Can you repeat your last name for me please?" At this point I decided to respond by spelling my name slowly and articulately as:

"M-A-P-E –P-A" I did this because I knew that the name sounded unusual to him because it was a foreign name and the sound was not familiar to his ear and hearing. The cop went on further to inquire and asked:

"What's your date of birth?" I gave him the answer. And his last question was:

"What's your social security number?"

I told him without any kind of hesitation or delay. His final words before exiting the Ambulance were:

"Thank you."

With these words, he jumped out of the ambulance and off he went away.

Once he'd jumped down, we took off in a great hurry towards the Hospital. The ambulance sped off in great speed with the sound of the siren blaring, blustering, and blasting through the cool twilight air.

The paramedic inside the ambulance assigned to attend to me continued asking further questions. The series of questions he asked were definitely deliberate, calculated and intentional. They were clearly intended to test my state of mind. He was examining me to make sure about my sobriety and consciousness and ascertain whether I was disoriented, confused or losing consciousness or just to test the soundness of my mind. In order to do this, he asked me questions like:

"What's the day today?" I answered him back and said,

"It's Wednesday." He went on to ask another question,

"What's the date today?" and I responded,

"It's the 9th of September, 2015." As if just to keep me engaged and awake, he pressed on with more questions among which he asked,

"What's your name?" Almost in a whisper, as I was slowly but quickly fading away due shallowness of breath, I answered,

"Steven."

To his surprise and satisfaction, I'd answered all his questions promptly, accurately, and correctly. In any case, I fully understood the purpose for him keeping me engaged, which made me even more alert and cautious in the way I answered. So, I made sure I prove to him I still had an alert and soundly conscious mind. Except that my voice was low and soft due to the degree of pain and the level of the overall deterioration of my condition and loss of breath. I was feeling weak and my voice had grown increasingly faint.

# CHAPTER THREE

Much earlier, at the accident scene, after calling Pastor Marvelous Ndhlovu, I'd also attempted to call my senior Pastor, papa Joshua florian Kamanda, but to no avail. My call had gone straight to his voicemail. Now, much later, while I was aboard the ambulance on my way to the Hospital, my phone rang, and it was him calling me back.

At this point, I'd drastically deteriorated. My physical condition had fallen to it's lowest ebb, I'd greatly declined. As I heard his voice from the other end, I quickly decided to inform him that I'd just got involved in a very serious car accident and I was fatally injured. I also told him that as I was talking to him I was aboard an ambulance being driven to Hospital.

Without any further delay I found it imperative to convey to him my last wishes before I could die. I said to him,

"Papa, I'm dying! Please take care of my wife and children because I'm at a point of death. I'm quickly running out of breath; so, if my voice fades away, and you hear that I've stopped talking, just know that I've died."

At this stage my voice was very low and soft, almost fading and falling into a whisper. He responded and told me that:

"My son, you shall not die! You shall live!" and he went on to say,"
I had clocked out and almost driving home, but I'll turn back and
wait for you."

As for me, I was almost about to finally clock out of this life and
go to my eternal home. Remember, I've mentioned to you before
that, Pastor Kamanda was not only my senior pastor, but also
a Chaplain at the Methodist Trauma Center Hospital in Indiana,
Indianapolis in the United States of America.

In fact, the Paramedic staff who was attending to me had asked
me earlier on:

"Where can we take you for treatment?"

"Eskenazi." I'd answered. Eskenazi is formerly Wishard Hospital
in down town Indianapolis. But the Paramedic had overruled my
choice of Hospital preference and had told me they were going
to take me to Indiana University Methodist Hospital. May be not
by coincidence according to divine providence, but by divine
appointment, because this is the same Hospital where my senior
pastor served as Chaplain.

As we were still talking my senior pastor asked me,

"Which Hospital are they taking you to?"

Since I'd been told by the Paramedic, I answered and told him,

Methodist Trauma center Papa!" and he responded and said,

"Ok, you'll find me here waiting for you."

At this point in time, the Paramedic was visibly agitated and
irritated by my being continuously on the phone. Having no more
patience with me, he ordered me and said:

"get off the phone sir, this is a very serious situation, you cannot continue being on the phone, cut off the phone and stop talking."

However, I went on to say my- would- be –final words of farewell to Papa. I said to him, "Papa, I'm dying! Once you hear me go quiet, just know I'm dead."

The paramedic raised his voice and retorted with a warning sound in his voice,

"Stop talking on the phone sir, this is not a joke!" Seeing the serious look on the face of the Paramedic and the anger in his voice, I said,

"Bye papa!" and I hang up.

The ambulance was cruising in high speed with the siren ringing out loud. This trip to the Hospital was really taking too long for me. This must have been largely to the amount of pain I was feeling plus the twists and turns the vehicle was taking.

Suddenly, I saw the Paramedic pull out a pair of scissors, and without hesitation, he went right on to cut through my pair of jeans, ripping through both my legs up to the waist, leaving me almost naked leaving me only with my underwear on. With a great amount of haste, he ripped off my skipper or T-shirt and left me lying bare to my skin on the stretcher.

At long last, we finally arrived at the Methodist Trauma Center Hospital, after what I seemingly felt like an ages long drive. Little did I know that the Paramedic had already made arrangements for my arrival at the Hospital well advance. Upon arrival I found a team of medical personnel already waiting for me. The medical team was well organized and prepared to start the job on the casualty. As soon as I arrived they wrapped me up and quickly moved me to another stretcher.

During all this process the pain in my body had become increasingly much more than I could bear. They quickly whisked me away to the Emergency Room. All these actions were done at great speed. The Leader of the Medical team issued brisk instructions that were carried out immediately without question or hesitation. I was taken to the X-ray and M.R.I- Magnetic resonating Imaging equipment. My body passed through these sophisticated machines that examined the minutest details of the internal injuries I had suffered. These pieces of equipment examined, assessed, and diagnosed the nature and extent of the internal injuries I had sustained.

When the findings were revealed, they were not only devastating but heart wrenching. With these new findings, the Medical team leader immediately recommended that they put a brace around my neck. The team immediately put a brace on me and also placed oxygen equipment on my nose. My whole body was filled with criss- crossing cords and patches to monitor my heart beat which was at the brink of stopping to beat. The bunch of cords attached to the equipment and my body were clear evidence of how critical my condition had become.

The Doctor told my Pastor Joshua Florian Kamanda who was also the Hospital Chaplain present, that I had suffered fatal and severe injuries than earlier anticipated. I'd sustained five broken ribs on the left side of my rib-cage, coupled with a broken collar-bone on the left shoulder. As if that was not enough, my left lung had been punctured, deflated and had collapsed losing its function at once. As if that was not enough, I'd also suffered two broken ribs on the right hand side of my rib-cage; fortunately, the right hand side lung was not pricked, punctured, deflated and collapsed leaving me with only one lung functioning and over worked. All together, I was left with seven broken ribs. As if that was not enough, I'd also suffered an overstretched vein on the left hand side of my neck. The vein had stuck out, strained, stretched, and swollen.

I was experiencing a combination of pain from various parts, positions, and sides of my body. To say the least, I was in terrible pain. The brace around my neck was exerting pressure on the lower side of my head causing excruciating pain and discomfort. I tried to tell the medical personnel attending to me to make necessary adjustments in order to ease the pain by putting a cushioning material around my head in order to mitigate and alleviate the pain. But, at this stage, I could hardly whisper. Eventually, I ceased and could not talk.

The Doctor heading the medical team, told Pastor and Chaplain Kamanda to start praying because chances for me to survive and live were very slim. Chances were that I could not make it. Because of this critical condition and situation, the Doctor said I couldn't make it to the operating room before the only other lung left and giving up would shut down completely and stop functioning. At that Stage, it will have been too late because my condition had drastically deteriorated. I'd have already died by the time they'd get me to the operating room for the surgery to be conducted.

The doctor had to make a decision in a split of a second, and indeed, he ordered that the surgery be conducted immediately in the Emergency Room there and then. According to the report and account given to me by my Senior Pastor J. Florian Kamanda, according to his own words, he saw the shadow of death over my face. At this juncture, Pastor Kamanda decided to send a group text to all our Church members and team of Pastors he leads called the "Eagles Pastors." This is a conglomerate team of Pastors under his leadership, each of these Pastors, was an autonomous leader of their own Ministries that chose to work together for a common cause that is to advance the work of the Kingdom of God in the city of Indianapolis, Indiana, They are the remnant churches of the ending times.

My Pastor frantically and vehemently started praying for me so that God would save my life and not let me die. At this moment I was desperately longing to be free from my own body riddled with fatal internal injuries and was in terrible pain. In other words, I was ready to exit out of my body which was in excruciating pain. I was ready and begging God to let me die.

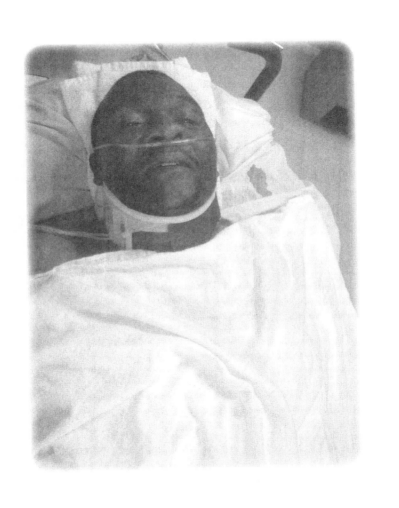

Indeed, at long last, I heard a click like sound, like a snap of a finger, I exited out of my body and transitioned into the outer realm and suddenly flipped into a spiritual atmosphere. I found myself on the flip side of life just like a coin turned from tells to King and I instantly became a spark and particle of light, and I heard myself pushing out a groaning sound and I said, uuhu! There was no break in my existence and instantaneously found myself before a much greater light. The greatest light ever known. I was before the light of all lights; this greater golden light was like the evening twilight of the setting African sun over the distant horizon. I was before that amazing light and I was feeling and knowing that I was connected to this greater life. This connection was wireless and I was a part of it.

At the point of exit or departure and transitioning to this realm, I felt an immense amount of relief and release from my painful mortal body which I was no longer a part of. I knew for sure and believed without the slightest shadow of a doubt that I'd died and passed on to another world. It might surprise you to know that my conclusion is that death is sweet release and a great relief. In no time and instantly I found myself before the divine, the sacred being. This being is what is called the ancient of days. This is the being that has no beginning and no ending. He is the one who was, who is, and will always be. He is the only being that was not created. He is the uncreated being, the self-existent, who is and is called and is known as: The I AM because He is. He is the one who exits and lives outside and beyond the limitations of time and occupies all space unimaginable. He is the all- knowing- omniscient God, everywhere, every time, He's the omnipresent-all present, everywhere and every time whom, even the whole wide space cannot contain. Amazingly, hard physical science-Astronomy attests to this infinite, all wise, immortal, all powerful, the everywhere and every time most intelligent being. The omnipotent God whose power no other being can contend. He's the invincible and invisible God, unseen by the physical and material realm of existence and all created things.

Surprisingly, I was much more alive, much more alert, and operating on a higher level of consciousness. I came to a deeper understanding of what Jesus Christ meant when He said: "I am the way, the truth, and the life. No one comes to the Father except through me." This is a verse found in the Holy Bible in the book of John 14:6. I knew that Besides Him and without Him there is nothing and no life. He is the sole source of life and all existence.

The level of reality and degree of consciousness was much higher and I was more alert and much more alive than I have ever known. There was no need for verbal communication. All forms of knowledge were intrinsically and inherently automatic and knowledge was freely flowing from this great light and source of divinely powerful being to me. While I was in His presence, I felt a kind of love and being loved like I have never been loved before. While in His presence I felt and knew a kind of peace, like I had never felt or known in my whole life, while in His presence, I felt such joy and happiness like I had never felt or known ever before. I felt a kind of compassion like I had never experienced before.

I felt and knew that I was back to my home where I was welcome and always longed to be. I've never felt such a sense of warm welcome. I was so overwhelmed by joy, peace, love, and compassion. I came to know and understand why the book of Psalms in the Holy Bible is full of songs of praises, exaltation, honor, prayers, powerful declarations, divine proclamations and decrees of magnifying this divine being I was now standing before. I understood why the Psalms in the holy Bible says: "Shout to the LORD." In His presence, and before this divine being, it's not a question of whether you want to shout or not; you are absolutely compelled to shout of his existence and glory. God exists and He is, there is no question about it. You don't shout because you want to, but because you have to, you have no other choice or option. It's the only alternative to express awe, wonder, admiration, gratitude, and thanksgiving. I comprehended that this is the mighty power that raised Jesus Christ, the Messiah, from the dead and caused Him to rise and be raised from the dead. In Him is the abundance of life and power exceeding all other powers that be. That's why the Holy Bible says: "In His presence, there is immense and exceeding light. He does not need light because He is the light and no need for the sun light, moonlight, and starlight. He is the ultimate and absolute light. REVELATIONS 22:5 "There will be no more light. They will not need the light of the lamp or the light of the sun, for the LORD God will give them light. And they will reign forever and ever." (NIV)

I was totally blown away by the nature of this supernatural spiritual being. I found myself in the spiritual and supernatural realm. It was another place, another realm, and indeed another very extraordinary environment like I have never imagined, experienced or seen before in my entire time of existence. I had exited and transitioned from the natural realm to the supernatural, from the physical to the spiritual, from the human form, to the divine form. I came from the mortal, and limited, to the immortal, and limitless, from the finite, to the infinite, from the here and now, to the hereafter and eternal form of existence.

The divine power of the sacred, holy word of the written word of God found in the Bible- the logos became evidently and suddenly alive. The Spirit kicked in and quickened my soul and transformed the logos word from mere information, knowledge and data, to a real personal life experience and turned it into a truly living experience. It became a Rhema word transfused, transmuted and infused in me the real absolute truth injecting in me sustaining living power into my frail, fragile, delicate, and deteriorating mortal dying body.

HEBREWS 4:12 says: "For the word of God is living and active. Sharper than any double-edged sword. It penetrates even to dividing soul and spirit, joints and marrow; it judges the thoughts and attitudes of the heart. Nothing in all creation is hidden from God's sight. Everything is uncovered and laid bare before the eyes of Him to whom we must give account." NIV

ISAIAH 55:11 Reinforces these words; and it says:

"so is my word that goes out from my mouth: It will not return to me empty, but will accomplish what I desire and achieve the purpose for which I sent it."

When you combine these two Holy Bible verses with JOHN 1:1; then, you will know that God is the word and the word has life and it is the light. Through it everything was created that is in existence. So, as for me, shouting and praising God was not a choice, but it was the only option and imperative.

The tragedy turned into a divine encounter with God of the universe and the pervasive absolute power that encompasses and covers all reality, existence, and all of creation. I remember that I began to shout in my inner being after I remembered that I'd been surrounded by a group of people who were attending to me before I'd exited and got out of my body and found myself before the divine power wrapped in a brilliantly shining light.

The reason I began to shout was to let them know that I was not only fully awake, alert, conscious, and alive in another realm beyond this immediate reality. Just in case they didn't know or believe that life doesn't end at the separation of this physical mortal body and the invisible soul which is immortal and infinite. I wanted for the medical team- both the Doctors and Nurses alike to know that I was alive with Jesus. I decided to report back to them all just in case they didn't know where I was.

The greater light which I was wirelessly connected to, began to move and transition to an unknown destination. As the light geared into motion I began to shout even more before I could disappear into the unknown endlessness.

This is the very core and crux of my story. This is the key moment of the entire course, purpose and meaning of this story of my life that depicts the real meaning behind this terrible car accident. Instead of being interpreted as a tragedy, it became a blessing in disguise, a spiritual treasure and a rare Medal of Honor. It became the birth of my ministry and message of what life means to me and a paradigm shift. I'm coming back from being transformed, transmuted after being touched by the divine. I'm coming back from a spark of light that became a flash of light at a click and snap of sound and suddenly went into transition and found life in a new and more real world, a new more immense and more alive reality. I found myself before a bright golden radiance- a bright light indeed like no other light can shine- the flip side of this present life. This new world had greater and more intense reality. The golden light is the divine one, and the sacred. According to me this is an aspect and characteristic of a living God.

REVELATION 21:23 says:

"The city does not need the sun or moon to shine on it, for the glory of God is light, and the lamb is its light." NIV

This is the reason I shouted: "Jesus is alive!" because I was before this radiant light. I was only testifying to the truth of where I was. I was confirming and affirming that Jesus is alive because I was truly before Him and with Him. I was making a proclamation and declaration as I decreed where I was. I was reporting what I was seeing and experiencing. I was before His presence. I was proclaiming the truth of my real life, or greater than life experience and reality before me and in me. Resulting from this experience of the divine encounter, I can solidly and truly attest, affirm, and confirm that Jesus is truly and absolutely alive. I'm speaking based on this real life experience and the faith I have always embraced all my life that culminated to this divine encounter.

Eventually, I began to hear my own voice and felt my own physical lips speaking these words with a great shout: "Jesus is alive!" From what I was told much later by my senior Pastor Kamanda, I'd been shouting out this declaration and proclamation on top of my voice for over twenty minutes and close to half an hour- thirty minutes. My voice had been echoing through the hallways, loud enough for all the Doctors and Nurses to hear, they were indeed baffled by this announcement and pronouncement.

Since this was a spiritual pronouncement, the medical team called the Chaplain, my senior Pastor to come and witness and try to make sense of what I was saying. My Pastor reported to me that I had my eyes closed and kept shouting on top of my voice. In fact, at one point I sensed some kind of commotion and opposition, as if someone somewhere was resisting my message of Jesus being alive. At this point, I remember wagging my index finger in the air saying: "No! No! No! My Jesus is alive. I said this in a defiant and matter of fact manner and tone. For me, this was an absolutely true reality and real life experience. I re-emphasized and reiterated my statement as one that was possessed by this divine presence and speaking as a witness of what I was experiencing and the true reality that was before me. My sensitivity had become high and augmented and a brand new world had opened to me. I was seeing and experiencing what nobody else could see or experience.

This, to me, was not a fantasy or figment of my imagination. It's concrete truth. It's an irrefutable and unquestionable report of what I saw and experienced. This account might sound subjective to other people who question things that concern faith and spiritual or supernatural experiences due to the fact that they are not visible, tangible, and objective. This is absolute truth to me. It is my personal spiritual experience and divine encounter. It augmented, substantiated, strengthened, and solidified my faith in the supernatural, divine, sacred, and invisible God.

# CHAPTER FOUR

In most cases and instances, the effects of anesthesia are viewed as forms of delusions and hallucinations. These unshared experiences are not seen or visible to others and hence are intrinsically subjective by their very nature. Most people do only believe what they see and what is physical, concrete and visible. This particular experience is objective, concrete and absolutely true to me which no one can dispute. If anyone thinks that this is just an opinion, but the least you can do is at least respect it even if you cannot prove it. Anyone is free to keep their misgivings and apprehensions. It is, and will always be my own personal experience and divine encounter that augmented, substantiated, strengthened and solidified my faith in the supernatural, spiritual, divine, and sacred invisible God to the naked physical eye.

However anyone may want to interpret it, for me, this is not an illusion, delusion, or hallucination. It is not a false perception. Usually, the effects of anesthesia can cause some people to say some incoherent things which do not make much sense. Mine was a clear and simply stated statement that: "Jesus is alive!" It does not matter to me what other explanation someone else may have about this experience, to me, and for me, it's the absolute truth.

When I reflect on the accident, many other potentially dangerous things would have happened, and different scenarios would have unfolded. Due to the bombardment and extent of the damage of the car crush, more fatal things would have happened that would have resulted in death. Firstly, any amount of gas leakage could have sparked a flame that could have turned into a blazing fire that would have engulfed us;

Consequently, that could have caused a burning fire that would have charred our bodies to ashes, and smoke that would have suffocated us to death. Especially that the car had become a mangled wreck that could not even enable us to exit from the-would- be burning car. Or else we could have all died at once. In another scenario, one of us, or even two could have died; me, my wife or the baby. Just think of how the aftermath of coping with any of these scenarios would have been.

We are so grateful to God for not allowing all of these hypothetical scenarios to happen. They didn't happen and we came out alive by the grace of God. In fact, analyzing our parallel conditions; on one hand, with me having sustained seven broken ribs, broken collar bone, and a punctured, deflated, and collapsed lung, with a yawning hole on the left side of my rib- cage with a pipe inserted inside of me in order to suck off the blood, fluids and prevent blood clots, I still wonder and stand in awe on how I could still shout audibly on top of my lungs: "Jesus is alive!"

after this initial surgery intended to resuscitate me by inflating my punctured, deflated and collapsed lung and inserting a tube to remove the blood and fluids that had drowned my lung, I was scheduled for a second surgery in order to straighten up and realign my broken bones- the seven broken ribs and a collar bone. Immediately after I was revived, I was personally very sad and disappointed to find out that I had come back to my physical body. Despite this, I still went on declaring that: "Jesus is alive!" for a while without stopping. But shortly afterwards, I began to ask: "But why? Jesus, why?" I was asking why he'd brought me back to this world, I'd temporarily left, and just to bring me back and redeposit me into this painful broken physical body when I'd already entered through the gates of glory and had stood before the light of eternity. In fact, I was asking why he'd allowed this kind of tragedy to happen to us.

As I gained my consciousness, my senior Pastor came over and squeezed my hand, and I looked up at him from my stretcher where I was lying and called out to him in unmistakable recognition and said: "Papa!" and he responded and said:

"All shall be well my son." In- a- matter- of- fact voice.

The medical team was on the scene and their leader issued instructions that I should be taken for a second assessment before they could conduct the second surgery that was intended to straighten up and align my broken ribs. After the MRI, the Doctor came back with exciting positive news that the lung had successfully got inflated and was functioning well again, and the other lung that had given up was fully operational and was working normally as well. This was good news and answered prayers by the saints who'd been praying for us.

I was immediately pushed way on my stretcher for the second MRI-Magnetic resonating Imaging. There I was again, I found myself going through a tunnel like piece of equipment with a visible bright light to the naked eye. After I came out and the Doctor reviewed the images from the MRI, and alas! The results were all the more encouraging and amazing. All my seven broken ribs on both sides of my rib cage and the collar bone were all back in alignment and in their original place. The Doctor announced once again, as another piece of good news that I didn't need a second surgery.

I don't know what you'd call this, but I call this a miracle at its best. All the broken bones were back in alignment and properly joined to their original positions. The collar bone was aligned and properly connected to its original position. The broken ribs were back in position and correctly and properly joined. That is what I define as a miracle- an act of God's divine power of intervention, not just the inflation and expansion of the rib-cage to its former state by way of just scientific explanation per se. At this point the Doctor ordered that I be taken to my Hospital bed and keep me in my room while work on pain management and mitigation of my long road to agony and recovery continued.

Throughout all this passage of time, I was on and off from sleep to being awake. my eyes would close and re- open intermittently. But at this particular time when I reopened my eyes I found Pastor Steven Cooper and his wife Josey looking down over me lying on the stretcher almost lifelessly. They'd rushed to the Hospital upon hearing that my wife and I had been involved in a fatal car accident.

They'd put everything else aside just to come and see us. I was so pleased to see them compassionately looking over me with all the sympathy I could see over their faces. They were accompanied by Papa Florian kamanda, and there, with him was our baby Dodo, safely in his arms. This was a great relief to me to see our baby safe, soundly healthy, alive and well and all this time she had just been calling out: "daddy! Daddy!" and the medical team had even asked why she called more of me than her Mom and Papa kamanda answered that it was because I spent a lot of time with her.

My most immediate next question was:" where's my wife? How's she doing?" and the answer papa gave me was: "She's fine and she's doing well." This settled my troubled mind because I'd not seen her since the last time I'd seen her in the car with a bulging swollen forehead. Each time I heard papa say:

"She's doing well, she's fine!"

Each time I heard these words I was comforted and relived to know that she was doing fine because I was continually worried about her condition and had asked these questions over and over to get assurance and reassurance.

I was not the only critically injured casualty in this terrible accident. As I came to learn later, my wife had suffered a broken spine- the part of the spinal code called C2 or the hanger-man's bone. This is a very fragile and delicate bone that could easily cause death or other fatal conditions. After she was examined by X-ray and MRI, the Doctor told her that this injury was a very serious one. It was the type that could potentially cause her either paralysis or a stroke once the surgery was done. He warned her that any slight mistake made to the veins would produce fatal results.

By all means this was a negative report, but instead, she quickly brushed this pessimistic view off her mind and decided to remain optimistic and hoped for positive results. She did not allow this report to trigger and instill fear, anxiety and worry in her. I thank God that she leaned on her faith instead of fear; she brushed aside all that sounded negative in her mind and ignited the spirit of faith in her as she brushed aside a negative report. Indeed, this perspective, helped her through it all. The Holy Bible says in HEBREWS 11:6 "And without faith it is impossible to please God, because anyone who comes to Him must believe that He exits and He rewards those who earnestly seek him."

This Rhema word became alive in her and worked the miracle that she desired. PSALMS 23:4 reinforces this and says: "Even though I walk through the valley of the shadow of death, I will fear no evil, for you are with me." Indeed, on the 10th of September, 2015 she underwent an amazingly successful Spinal cord surgery where she emerged exonerated by her faith in a God who hears prayers and rewards those who not only believe in Him, but also seek Him earnestly. She neither suffered a stroke nor had paralysis. She came out intact, only with a brace around her neck. This was yet another miracle! A double miracle! God had rescued both of us from death or any other form of tragedy contrary to conventional knowledge, predictions, and wisdom. This was a manifestation of God's divine wisdom. We both feared no evil for God was with us. We answered the critical question which says: "Whose report shall you believe?" we chose to believe God's report that is in the book of ISAIAH 53:3-5 "He was despised and rejected by men, a man of sorrows, and familiar with suffering. Like one from whom men hide their faces he was despised, and we esteemed him not. Surely he took up our infirmities and carried our sorrows, yet we considered him stricken by God, smitten by him, and afflicted. But he was pierced for our transgressions, he was crushed for our iniquities; the punishment that brought us peace was upon him, and by his wounds we are healed."

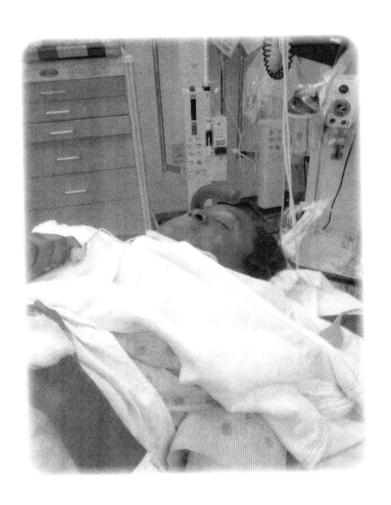

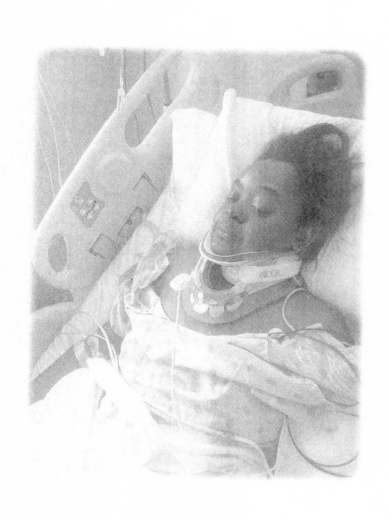

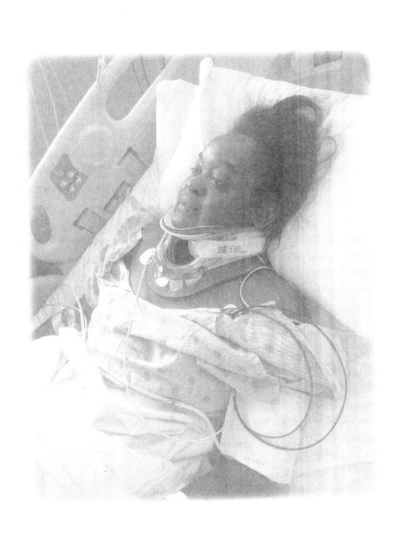

Jesus Christ is our defender, our God is the tower of our strength, he is our cave and refuge. This car accident had gone way too far, so much so that my wife had also passed out and when she came to her consciousness she'd asked:

"What happened?" the paramedic attending to her answered,

"You're involved in a car accident!" When she was told this, she began declaring and proclaiming positive words of gratitude saying:

"Thank you Jesus! Thank you Jesus!" This is a strange and contradictory response right? These are unusual similarities to the way we responded to this tragedy. We both declared the name of Jesus. Truly there's power in the name of Jesus.

Before this tragedy had occurred, our senior pastor JF Kamanda had put my wife and I on a process of deliverance coupled with a long stretch of fasting and praying. We'd fasted and prayed for over five months, and close to six months. In our reflections and review of the accident, we came to a common conclusion and agreement that our deliverance process, fasting and praying were a spiritual investment whose dividends had a lot to do with touching God's heart, which caused God all the more to look out for us in very extraordinary and supernatural ways.

We had in essence prayed against the spirit of death due the various dreams my wife had had. In our prayers we were binding, breaking, destroying, casting down and away, refusing, resisting, opposing, neutralizing, rendering ineffective and powerless, nullifying, cancelling, disowning, and divorcing all the spiritual attacks from the kingdom of darkness. We were engaged in what is known as spiritual warfare in the Christian circles. We were disconnecting, removing, crushing and dismantling all the plans, schemes, projects, and strategies of the enemy. We were closing doors to demonic influences, attacks, oppression, possession, and any assignments of the devil's errands and intentions of destruction.

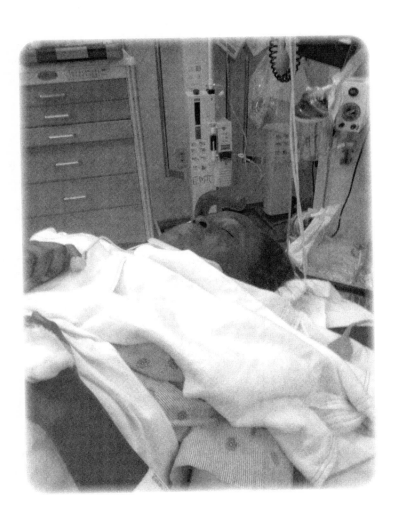

The devil's ministry, mission, and vision are found in the Holy Bible's book of JOHN 10:10 which says: "The thief comes only to steal and kill and destroy;" but Jesus says: "I have come so they may have life, and have it to the full." In this case the devil had stolen, crushed, and destroyed our car, intending to break our bodies in pieces and kill us. Doctor Joseph Choga who is a Physical therapist, a Minister of the Gospel and Medical Doctor Student on the Caribbean Union Island told us that what my wife had broken, the C2 was also called the Hanger man's bone which the devil had intended to break which qualifies him to be a murderer.

JOHN 8:44 further confirms this assertion and Jesus said:

"You belong to your father, the devil, and you want to carry out your father's desire. He was a murderer from the beginning, not holding to the truth, for there is no truth in him. When he lies, he speaks his native language, for he is a liar and the father of lies."

This is the stark difference and contrast between Jesus and the devil. Jesus is the way, the life and the truth, while the devil is a murderer, liar, and thief. My wife and I proclaimed the Jesus who is the life. He is the word, the light and power through whom everything in existence was created. Jesus is God because God the Father is in Him and He is in the Father with the Holy Spirit forming the Godhead- three in one or simply the Trinity. In essence the Trinity is one God who is three persons in one- The Father, the son, and the Holy Spirit. This is the Almighty God who rescued us miraculously.

This miracle of our rescue became clear evidence of our deliverance. We were delivered, rescued, saved and redeemed from bloodline curses, genealogical curses, family line and family tree curses, generational and personal curses which might have been caused by our own sinful nature. We have sinned through our own thoughts, words, and deeds. We might have opened doors all by our own doing, our own faults that might have allowed the devil to come in. Our God kicked him out and defeated him.

We were delivered! We are forever grateful souls in the redemptive power of Jesus our LORD according to the words that come out of our mouths. This is the power found in the name of Jesus our King. PROVERBS 18:21 says: "The tongue has the power of life and death, and those who love it will eat its fruit." NIV. That is the power of words, as the Holy Bible says that the power of life and death lies in the words of your mouth. What you speak in the atmosphere is what you create and it is expressed through physical manifestations. PROVERBS 23:7 says: "For as he thinks in his heart, so is he." NKJV. This simply means that as a man thinks, so is he. So, what you think is what you are. If you have studied Psychology, you might have heard of what is called: The self-fulfilling prophecy." Also that there are three levels of the mind according to Sigmund Freud, and these are: The unconscious level of the mind, also called the ID, the subconscious, also known as the ego, and the Conscious also known as the super-ego stratum of the mind. These strata are all interconnected and intertwined. So, what you feed your mind with is ultimately what you produce. What goes inside of your mind is what comes out of you and makes who you are. These are the consequences of what we entertain and harbor in our minds. It is also proved through a method of therapy called Psychotherapy where a subject or patient goes through hypnothesis. The patient is put in deep sleep and begins to speak while they are in a trance or dream like state as it is done in the use of anesthesia.

The point I'm making is, what is embedded, enshrined, engraved, and imprinted in your mind is what you speak out even if you are in a state of sleep or even in dreams. Whatever information or data that your mind has received as knowledge is what forms your "mental- DNA," and that's what you ultimately express. It becomes the core of your DNA. If I may use the analogue of a computer; what is in your mind, soul, heart, and spirit, is your "mental- software" that is expressed and comes out through your "physical- hardware" which is your mouth or lips as parts of your physical body.

This was proved by our testimony after the fatal crush. I declared the proclamation and cried out in awe praising and decreeing that: "Jesus is alive!" after I had crossed over to another realm and spiritual dimension; and my wife on the other side also as she was rising from passing out. Ironically, contrary to normal expectations she began to thank Jesus for the horrible and terrible accident. This is the evidence of our spiritual software expressed through our physical hardware- the lips of our mouths that spoke out the words of life as opposed to death. ACTS 17:28 says: "For in him we live and move and have our being; as some of your own poets have said, 'We are his offspring.' NIV

We do not have an independent form of existence; we owe our existence, lives, and our very being in him. Without him there is no life because he is the sole source of life, and there is no other source apart from him and him alone. The Holy Bible also says in the book of ROMANS 10:8 "But what does it say? The word is near you; it is in your mouth and in your heart, that is the word of faith we are proclaiming. That if you confess with your mouth, "Jesus is Lord," and believe in your heart that God raised him from the dead, you will be saved. For it is with your heart that you believe and are justified, and it is with your mouth that you confess and are saved. As the scripture says, "Anyone who trusts in him will never be put to shame. For there is no difference between Jew and Gentile- The same Lord is the Lord of all and richly blesses all who call on him, for, everyone who calls on the name of the Lord will be saved."

This is true salvation in action. Salvation is not fiction or an illusion but a reality. This is redemption manifested in this day and age in our present generation. Salvation transcends time, era, and dispensation. The grace of God is always at work, and grace works. I'm glad that through our tragedy, I can confidently say we live it, we experience it, we see it, we believe it, and we receive it as a gift from God. We do not earn it. It is unmerited favor, it is undeserved, and for that we are grateful souls and forever grateful in our hearts. We are saved by his grace. The power of grace is working, now in this moment and for as long as the Lord gives it.

HEBREWS 11:1 says: "Now faith is being sure of what we hope for and certain of what we do not see. This is what the ancients were commended for. By faith we understand that the universe was formed at God's command, so that what is seen was not made out of what was visible." My wife and I believed in things we could not see. God did not let our hope down. He did not disappoint us or bring us to shame for calling out his name. Surely our attendants must have thought we were crazy to call upon a God who had let us down by failing to prevent the accident. I'm sure that they were wondering what kind of God would allow his children to be subjected to such misfortune, calamity, and pain. But our God works in mysterious ways and turns the bad things for our good. If this did not happen, how could we share this testimony for other souls to know there is a miracle working God? What a mighty, good, and merciful God we serve!

We are recipients and beneficiaries of his grace, mercy, compassion and miracles. We are the evidence of his incomparable power and goodness. This is our story.

# CHAPTER FIVE

The teaching and learning drawn from this tragedy bore the birth of this song and brought its words to life. My Anthem is found in the lyrics of the song whose text was written by Fanny J. Crosby-1820-1915 and the music by Phoebe P. Knapp-1839-1908. The title of the song is:

BLESSED ASSURANCE

1. BLESSED ASSUARNCE
   JESUS IS MINE
   O WHAT A FORETASTE OF GLORY DIVINE
   HEIR OF SALVATION, PURCHASED OF GOD
   BORN OF HIS SPIRIT, WASHED IN HIS BLOOD
   REFRAIN
   THIS IS MY STORY, THIS IS MY SONG
   PRAISING MY SAVIOR ALL THE DAY LONG
   THIS IS MY STORY, THIS IS MY SONG
   PRAISING MY SAVIOR ALL THE DAY LONG
   REFRAIN:

2. PERFECT SUBMISSION, PERFECT DELIGHT
   VISIONS OF RAPTURE NOW BURST ON MY SIGHT
   ANGELS DESCENDING, BRING FROM ABOVE
   ECHOES OF MERCY, WHISPERS OF LOVE
   REFRAIN:
   REFRAIN:

3. PERFECT SUBMISSION, ALL IS AT REST
   I IN MY SAVIOR AND HAPPY AND BLEST
   WATCHING AND WAITING, LOOKING ABOVE
   FILLED WITH HIS GOODNESS, LOST IN HIS LOVE.
   REFRAIN:

This is my story. This is our story with my wife, family, relatives, and friends. This is our story; this is our song praising our savior, all the day long because we are so full of gratitude to be alive. To be given yet another chance to live. Life, to us, is a sacred gift from the divine and sacred God of providence, provision, protection, and unending ocean of compassion. Life, to us, is a privilege and not a right because it belongs to the Lord our God who can give and take it away. Life can be withdrawn at any time by him who gives it and takes it way; hence, we're forever grateful souls.

Our story cannot end without mentioning the time or duration of our unusually short time we were admitted and stayed in Hospital. With all this severity of injuries and surgeries, my wife was the first one to be discharged from Hospital on the fourth day after the fateful day of our accident. We had the accident on the 9th of September, 2015 which was a Wednesday, and she was discharged four days later on a Saturday, which was the 12th of September, 2015. But before that, she'd called on me in order to find out how I was doing. When she called on me, we chatted and updated each other on how our physical conditions were.

I came to know that she didn't know my physical condition in the initial days of our admission into Hospital. She actually told me that she thought I was ok and had not been fatally injured. Moreover, she told me that she was just wondering why I was not calling to check on her. In her own words, she said:

"I was actually mad at you that you were not calling or coming over to check on me." But when she heard about my injuries, she was not only shocked, but also filled with feelings of concern and was eager to know how I was doing. She was relieved after speaking to me and hearing the story from me. Though she was discharged in the morning, she only got home much later after midnight.

On the following day, which was the fifth day, the 13th of September, 2015, the Doctor came to my admission room with his medical team on the usual routine to check on my condition. The Doctor made his usual assessment, but to his surprise, something was not quite right. Just to discover that the tube they had inserted in me on the left hand side of my rib cage, just under my breast and close to my arm pit, was in fact, not in the right position to continue suctioninig the excess blood and fluids due to internal bleeding. Upon dicovering this anomaly, the Doctor made an immediate decision to have it removed. He told his team that my natural body functions would be capable of absorbing the excess blood and fluids.

The whole team left in order to prepare for the removal of the tube. Surprisingly, upon her return, the female junior Doctor who was part of the team, returned alone to my Hospital admission cubical with some amazing news. She came and announced that I was ready to go home and continue with the healing process. I had spent only five days in Hospital; and guess what? Five, is a divine number of grace and the chronological position of my birth in the line of my siblings. I'm the fifth child among thirteen children my mother and father had. After announcing this good news, she started the process of removing the tube. I was expecting the worst agony, but to my surprise, it was so easy. The tube just simply dropped off without much effort as if someone had already been pulling it out slowly. I was relieved.

The junior Doctor bandaged and covered my fresh wound and signed the discharge papers and I was free to go home. Fortunately, my dearest wonderful friend Martin Landwerlen was right on hand to give me a ride home. I did not have to look for someone to come over from some distance somewhere and drive me home. This, to me, yet again, was not a coincidence of events but God's providencial arrangement. This was divine intervention and and provision.

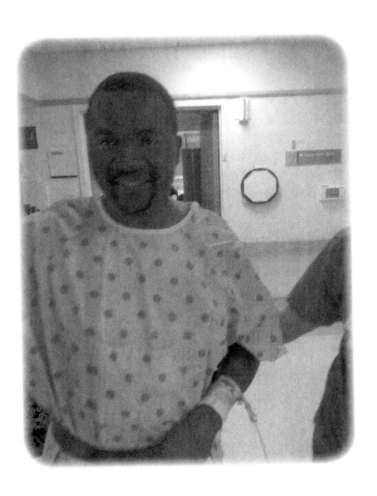

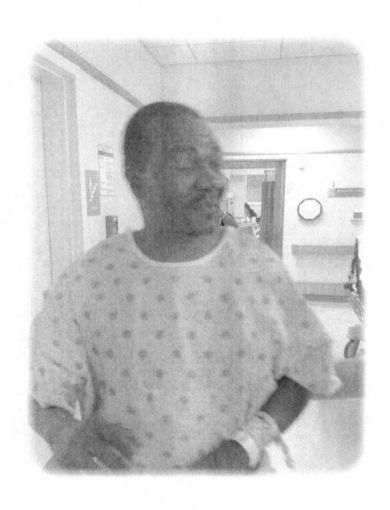

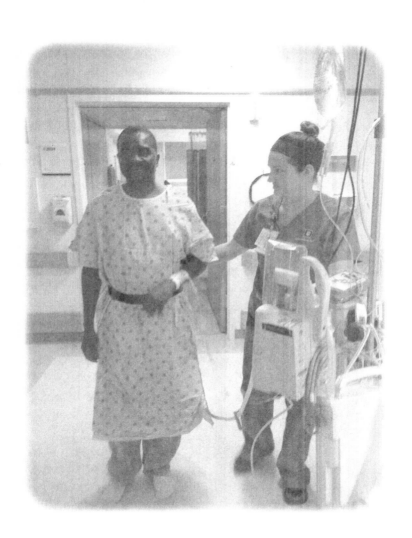

Indeed, that very morning, still dressed in my Hospital attire, since my own clothes had been ripped by the Paramedic, I went home and had a wonderful time chatting with my friend Martin on my way home.

My physical condition was still fragile, and delicate. I was feeling and looking frail. Thanks to God, my wife, friends, and children gave me the needed and necessary support. My ten year old son, Rungano, was holding my hand regularly to give the needed support to get me up because I couldn't get up on my own due to the broken bones and the agony of pain. My sleeping was extremely difficulty since I couldn't sleep on both of my sides due to the multi fractured ribs on both sides of my rib cage. This was a very hard time for both my wife and I.

There were a few natural reflex actions I feared should not have to happen namely: sneezing, coughing, and hiccups because of the fragility and pain they would cause to my broken ribs as any of these reflexes would cause my rib cage to expand and contract in quick motions. Remember, I was in the initial stage and process of mending. This was a very tough phase on its own. Glory to God, because none of these natural reflex actions ever happened at this delicate phase until much later in the second month when my bones were strong enough to deal with those movements. This time it could not hurt so much to sneeze or cough. I did these things with a lot of caution. We entered the third month which the Doctor told me was the final healing phase. Thank God! No hiccups and no cough.

As we entered the third month, I was feeling almost completely healed. It was somewhere around the third week or early second month after the accident that I went back to work and started driving again. On the other hand, my wife demonstrated a lot of courage, endurance, perseverance, and amazing faith. She was on the go immediately after leaving Hospital. She was a moving and working miracle. Unlike me, she never really rested to recuperate. She was always on the go and on the move. She was doing even harder chores and things even much more than before. To be honest, I really feared for her, but her unflinching, unwavering determination surprised me. She showed much more acts of faith than I did. This, to me, was not only encouraging, but also challenging indeed. What a mighty God we serve who enabled her to do all the things she did.

We're both glad to be alive, safe, sound, and strong until now. We can declare that we're healed in Jesus' name. We're both safely out of danger. We're on safer and higher ground, in our physical bodies, emotions, faith, spiritual lives and general well being. We've emerged stronger, wiser, and firmly standing on our faith in the Lord, the God who recued and saved us out of the terrible, horrible, and otherwise fatal car accident. All glory goes to our God for His mercies that are new every morning. The Bible, in the book of LAMENTATION 3: 22-23 says: "Because of the LORD'S great love we are not consumed, for His compassions never fail. They are new every morning; great is your faithfulness. I say to myself, "The LORD is my portion; therefore I will wait for him. The LORD is good to those who hope in him, to the one who seeks him; it is good to wait quietly for the salvation of the LORD." Glory is to our God!

I also made a very interesting observation and discovery. I call this a divine revelation. The place, form, and shape of the accident scene was at a four way intersection. The four way intersection creates the shape of a cross where Jesus Christ our messiah was crucified and took away all the sins of the world. All curses, devils and demons on mankind were lifted up and nailed to the cross. Ultimately, death was conquered on the cross through the ultimate sacrifice for all humanity. Hence, this was proved by the evidence of the declarations and proclamations that my wife and I decreed in our dying moments. My wife declared, proclaimed, and decreed saying: "Thank you Jesus!" and I cried out saying: "Jesus is alive!" we became the mouthpiece of the message of redemption. We declared the message of salvation even in death knowing that Jesus conquered all for us and claimed our lives from the mouth of the roaring lion the devil.

The word of life was right there on the lips of our mouths. We spoke life and God gave us the life that he used to resurrect His son Jesus Christ the power of creation as it is written in JOHN 1:1 which says: "In the beginning was the word, and the word was with God. He was with God in the beginning. Through Him all things were made; without him nothing was made that has been made. In him was life, and that life was the light of men. The light shines in the darkness, but the darkness has not understood it." And when we skip and go to verse 10, we read, "he was in the world, and though the world was made through Him, the world did not recognize him. He came to that which was his own, but his own did not receive him, yet to all who received him, to those who believed in his name, he gave the right to become children of God- children born not of natural descent, nor of human decision or a husband's will, but born of God. The word became flesh and made his dwelling among us. We have seen his glory, the glory of the one and only, who came from the Father, full of grace and truth."

This is how powerful the word is. It is almighty! It is All knowing, and all present, God with us- Emmanuel. So, when we call upon Jesus, we're calling the all powerful God full of life and light. He gave us the right, not the privilege to be called the children of God. Therefore when I saw the golden glow of light I saw a glimpse of the foretaste of glory divine. Jesus is the totality and full embodiment of all that was created because all things were created through him. The records and accounts of the physical universe are all a manifestation of Jesus as it is written in the accounts of creation when God spoke all things into existence by the power of the word of His mouth, his one and only son Jesus Christ. The account of GENESIS 1:1-NIV when God says: "Let there be light and there was light!" "The let there be's" in Genesis reaffirm this account by JOHN 1:1. NIV

These two books of the Holy Bible speak of the one exact account of the beginnings and creation. The meaning is self- explanatory and does not need any mental or intellectual gymnastics or flips. It is as simple and straightforward and easy to understand as it is stated and recorded. It is loud and clear that all things were created by the voice of God that spoke all things into existence. The book of John says the word was with God and was God and he was with Him in the beginning and that all things were created through the word. Similarly, the Book of Genesis records the account of creation as a spoken word from God, when God said, "Let there be light, there was light, and whatever the power of His word spoke came into existence all at once without any time lapse or delay. There was instant appearance of whatever He spoke at the command of His word. There is no further debate, argument, of deeper interpretation required. It is not implicit and does not contain any figurative, dark, or hidden meaning. It is not a riddle, parable, or proverb. It means just exactly what it says, as it says it. Dead simple right?

The story of creation does not require unnecessary disputes. It has no disagreements or contradictions, but the purely absolute true word of God. Everything was made through the one and only son of God, Emmanuel whose literal meaning is God with us who came and lived among us- Jesus the Christ, our Messiah, King, Master, and savior who who took the fall on the cross to claim His own to Himself and reconcile all the estranged children to their rightful and legitimate Father-God. Jesus Christ is the word that became flesh and took the form of a human being who did extraordinary things ever recorded in human history. The only one who resurrected from the dead and ascended to Heaven in full view of onlookers. Jesus is the life, he is the light, and He is God. How much more simpler can this be explained in order to be understood in the easiest terms? How else can Jesus' story and deity be told?

This tragic, terrible, horrible, and fatal car accident we were involved in ignited and augmented the realness of the word of the word of God. The word became the life, the light, and the truth with grace as recorded in the book of John.

# CHAPTER SIX

In my closing segment, I will carefully select some verse extracts, synopses, and gleanings in how the word of God, written in the Holy Bible, came to be so alive to me as confirmed in the book of HEBREWS 4:12 which says: "For the word of God is living and active. Sharper than any double-edged sword, and it penetrates even to dividing soul and spirit, joints and marrow; it judges the thoughts and attitudes of the heart. Nothing in all creation is hidden from God's sight. Everything is uncovered and laid bare before the eyes of him to whom we must give account." And ISAIAH 55:11-NIV, which reiterates what the preceding verse just asserted, and God says about His word: "So is my word that goes out of my mouth: It will not return to me empty, but will accomplish what I desire and achieve the purpose for which I sent it." These two verses are confirmed by the recorded word in JOHN 1:1-14, and GENESIS 1:1-31.NIV

To me, the word of God instantly transformed from being just logos, or mere information, knowledge, and data, but became alive; a Rhema word that has life and real demonstration of power of raising the dead to life, both in the physical and spiritual realms, in the natural and the supernatural, in both the ordinary and extraordinary, in the now and the hereafter, in the finite and limited, to the infinite and unlimited, in the mortal and immortal realms, in the human and divine forms and dimensions, in the lower and the higher levels.

I am so grateful to Jesus my King, my LORD, and Master. I am so thankful and deeply indebted to God, our father, and the Holy

Ghost, who rescued us from the cold hand of death. The blood of the Lamb was smeared on the door posts of our lives so that the angel of death would pass us over as in the plagues of Egypt. This was the blood of the lamb, our savior Jesus Christ. God caused our minds, souls, spirits, and our very being, to praise Him in the midst of pain, suffering, loss, agony, and death. Our God caused us to speak life in spite of being face to face with calamity, misfortune, tragedy, and potentially imminent death. We were under siege and the strong grip of death.

I testify to being released back from death, to this physical, natural, earthly life. My wife, daughter, and I are alive all by the grace of God. We believe that we were saved so that we could come back and accomplish the unfinished work which God preordained and predestined for us. We are sure that we are here on assignment and on a mission in this natural physical earthly realm before moving on to the spiritual and eternal home.

Here is the list of well selected scriptures of the Rhema word and how it directly relates to our situation and tragic story:

2 CORINTHIANS 4: 7-NIV "But we have this treasure in the jars of clay to show that this all surpassing power is from God and not from us. We are hard pressed on every side, but not crushed, perplexed, but not in despair; persecuted, but not abandoned, struck down, but not destroyed. We all carry around our body the death of Jesus, so that the life of Jesus may also be revealed in our body. For we who are alive are always being given over to death for Jesus sake, so that his life may be revealed in our mortal body. So then, death is at work in us, but life is at work in you.

It is written: "I believed; therefore I have spoken. With that same spirit of faith we also believe and therefore speak, because we know that the one who raised the Lord Jesus from the dead will also raise us with Jesus and present us with you in his presence. All this is for your benefit, so that the grace that is reaching more and more people may cause thanksgiving to overflow the glory of God.

Therefore we do not lose heart. Though outwardly we are wearing away, yet inwardly we are being renewed day by day. For our light and momentary troubles are achieving for us an eternal glory that far outweighs them all. So we fix our eyes not on what is seen, but what is unseen. For what is seen is temporary, but what is unseen is eternal."

This living word is clearly and explicitly confirming that we are but just jars of clay that can be easily broken like dry clay and inevitably wasting away in decay. In fact, our car and ourselves were broken. We were hard pressed from all the sides of the road and hit by other cars, and our bodies almost crushed, but we were not destroyed. The same invisible and invincible mystery of the supernatural spiritual power of God rescued us and restored both our bodies and lives to stay alive. The all surpassing power from God who is the light and the life, as the scripture is saying explicitly expressed. The same power that raised Christ from the dead also delivered and raised us from the dead to life. Our God defended us from death. We responded with hearts of thanksgiving overflowing by us preaching the message of Christ to the medical personnel while we were being operated on upon the operation tables. We preached to the Doctors and nurses, and all the medical staff present there and all those who heard us proclaim and declare the good news and name of Jesus.

Everyone who heard the declarations and proclamations of the decrees about Jesus that my wife and I made as she said: "Thank you Jesus!" while faced with a great probability of a stroke or potential paralysis on one hand, and I, faced with death on the other, but still shouting on the operation table that: "Jesus is alive!" Jesus said, if you acknowledge Him in public, He, too, will acknowledge you in front of His Father in heaven. He, who is in us, is greater than he who is in the world. All this happened to us so that God would get all the glory. Like I said already, the real hero is not the rescued, but the rescuer. We, who were rescued, do not deserve any praise, honor, or glory, but God who rescued us deserves all the praise, honor and glory. God is the true hero, and we are not heroes by any measure.

Though this tragic calamity would have been intended by the evil one to break us, but God actually turned it for good. God caused us to emerge stronger, wiser, and firmer in our faith which remained rock-solid through this entire horrific ordeal. He saw us through it all. We went through it all thanking and praising the name of the rock of ages who made us cheat death, as we narrowly escaped it so that we could tell our story and serve Him.

REVELATION 12:10-NIV says:

"Then I heard a loud voice in Heaven say: Now has come the salvation and the power and the kingdom of our God, and the authority of his Christ. For the accuser of our brothers, who accuses them before our God day and night, has been hurled down. They overcame him by the blood of the lamb and the word of their testimony."

This is our story. It is our triumph over the enemy. We overcame him by the blood of the Lamb, and now, we are sharing the word of our testimony. We emerged victorious! The Holy Bible says, the wicked one is like a roaring lion seeking who to devour because he knows that his time is short. He wanted to devour us, but our God defended us and stood strong for us. Remember how Satan went before God, and in their dialogue accused Job, a righteous man in God's sight, and how consequently, he tormented him.

JOB 42:1-6-NIV

Then Job replied to the Lord, I know that you can do all things, no plan of yours can be thwarted. You asked, 'Who is this one who obscures my counsel without knowledge?' Surely I spoke of things I did not understand, things too wonderful for me to know. You said, listen now and I will speak; I will question you, and you shall answer me. My ears had heard of you but my eyes have seen you. There I despise myself and repent in dust and ashes." Hence, we give thanks and glory to God, for He is good all the time in all seasons and all times.

ROMANS 5:1-NIV

"Therefore, since we have been justified through faith, we have peace with God through our Lord Jesus Christ, through whom we have access by faith into this grace in which we now stand. And we rejoice in the hope of the glory of God. Not only so, but we also rejoice in our suffering, because we know that suffering produces perseverance, perseverance, character, and character, hope. And hope does not disappoint us, because God has poured out his love into our hearts by the Holy Spirit, whom he has given us. You see, just at the right time, when we were still powerless, Christ died for the ungodly." But God demonstrates his own love for us in this: while we were still sinners, Christ died for us."

This is the irony and paradox in the walk of faith. Isn't it amazing that we have to rejoice in our suffering? Just think of it if someone told you to rejoice in your sufferings. Isn't this a paradox? Indeed, the irony is that through all this God is glorified through our sufferings because He is a good Father who teaches us perseverance through suffering, and builds character in us through our troubles. Our character creates hope and inspires the ignition of the Holy Ghost whom he has given us. Our God is good and has no evil plans for anyone of us. He has only good plans. We might have dark days and seasons riddled with problems and afflictions, but He has all the power to turn it all for good. God our Father has good plans for all His children who trust in Him and has no evil intentions whatsoever, as he says in His Holy word in the book of:

JEREMIAH 29:11-14-NIV

"For I know the plans I have for you," declares the LORD, "plans to prosper you and not to harm you, plans to give you hope and a future. Then you will call me and find me when you seek me with all your heart. I will be found by you," declares the LORD." This is a declaration, not a claim. Let us call on Him and seek Him with all our hearts and we will find Him.

JAMES 1:2-3-NIV

"Consider it pure joy, my brothers, whenever you face trials of many kinds, because you know that the testing of your faith develops perseverance. Perseverance must finish its work so that you may be mature and complete, not lacking anything. If any of you lacks wisdom, he should ask God, who gives generously to all without finding fault, and will be given to him. But when he asks he must believe and not doubt, because he who doubts is like the wave of the sea, blown and tossed by the wind. That man should not think he will receive anything from the LORD, he is double-minded, unstable in all he does."

Suffering, trials and tribulations, perseverance, endurance, persistence and insistence, creates maturity and wisdom in us. That is why I say coming out of the car accident; we emerged stronger, wiser, and firmer in our walk of faith with Christ Jesus. It helped us more much more than hurt us. God's ways are incomprehensible and he works in mysterious ways. The devil might have meant it for bad, but God turned it for our good, just as the Holy Bible account recorded in the story of Joseph and his brothers who intended to hurt him and all things turned out for his good according to God's plan for his destiny. God can turn all situations, circumstances, and events for our good and for His glory. We must count our tragedies and calamities as blessings in disguise and give all the glory to God who deserves it.

ROMANS 8:28-30- NIV

"And we know that in all things God works for the good of those who love him, who have been called according to his purpose. For those God foreknew he also predestined to be conformed to the likeness of his son, that he might be the first born among many brothers. And those he predestined, he also called, those he called, he also justified, those he justified, he also glorified."

Our struggles are against negative forces running in opposition against us and the battles we face do intensify their resistance against us; but we must continue to press on and endure the pain. We must always know that; he who is in us is greater than the one who is in the world who is relentlessly fighting against us. He is working over time because he knows that his time is fast running out and growing shorter by the day. We must keep believing and knowing that in all things (not some), but all things, God works for the good of us who love him and have been called according to His purposes.

Therefore, we need to be in one accord with His purpose, will, calling and destiny because he foreknew us long before we came into existence. He called us to be among many of His children with Jesus Christ His son as the first born among them all. Predestination means that God already knew us prior to creating us and He had already had a plan or a mission for us to accomplish in this life. Our destiny is God's dream, vision, assignment, task, and mission for us to do on this earth to His glory. Through Jesus Christ, we are justified by God's grace and the blood of Jesus that cleansed us from our sins, transgressions, iniquities, and flaws. We have been set apart to do His work for His glory. I thank God over and over again that my wife, daughter, and I did not die in that car accident because God has a purpose, calling, and work for us to finish in the remaining days of our lives on this earth before we finally go home to live with Him eternally. We were preserved for an assignment we need to complete for Him. I believe He gave us this testimony so that we could share it and cause others to know Him and be saved.

We know and believe that God knows each one of us and loves us individually and collectively. He knew each one of us before we were born as He told Jeremiah and David. The first account of predestination is found in the book of JEREMIAH 1:5-(NIV) where God said to Jeremiah:

"Before I formed you in the womb I knew you, before you were born, I set you apart, I appointed you as a Prophet to the nations."

In the same way that God knew Jeremiah before He formed him in the womb, and before he was born, God knew him and set him apart and appointed him as a Prophet to the nations. Therefore, each one of us is special and uniquely created by God for a specific purpose that should give God the glory. We may not all be called to be Prophets, but surely, each one of us was created for a special and unique reason we each have to accomplish and give account to God when our day is done on this earth. Our God is an omniscient God. He knows everything at all times, in all places. I do believe that God foresaw even this fateful day of the accident long before it ever happened and it was already recorded long before it came to be. We thank God for His grace and not our works. He spared us from death and we are blessed to be still alive even to be able to give this rare testimony and share it so that He is not only glorified but that His children should come to know Him as a living God who knows everything and is forever in control of all our lives and situations.

In the book of PSALMS 138:8 the Holy Bible says:

"The LORD will fulfill his purpose for me; (with your right hand you save me.) Your love, O LORD endures forever- do not abandon the works of your hands."

PSALMS 139:1

O LORD you have searched me, and you know me when I sit down and when I rise, you perceive my thoughts from afar, you discern my going out and my lying down; you are familiar with all my ways. Before a word is on my tongue, you know it completely O LORD. You hem me in behind and before; you have laid your hand upon me. Such knowledge is too wonderful for me, too loft for me to attain. Where can I go from your Spirit? Where can I flee from your presence? If I go up to the Heavens, you are there, if I make my bed in the depths, you are there. If I rise on the wings of the dawn, if I settle on the far side of the sea, even there your hand will guide me, your hand will hold me fast. If I say surely the darkness shall hide me and light became night around me, even the darkness will not be dark to you, the night will shine like the day, for darkness is as light to you. For you created my inmost being, you knit me together in my mother's womb. I praise you because I am fearfully and wonderfully made; your works are wonderful. I know that full well. My frame was not hidden from you when I was made in the secret place. When I was woven together in the depths of the earth. Your eyes saw my unformed body. All the days ordained for me were written in your book before one of them came to be."

This whole chapter confirms that God is all knowing. He is an omniscient God. He is omnipresent, he is everywhere every time; there is nowhere in the universe where His presence is not. He saw the frames of our bodies even before they were made. His eyes saw our unformed bodies, and as we walk in our future, to God, we are walking into the past. As we are walking into our destiny, to God, we are walking in our history. What is brand new to us, is very old to God-the ancient of days. Everything ordained for each one of us was already written in His book of life before any one of them came to be. He is an all powerful God- He is omnipotent and no one can conquer Him or defeat His plans for each one of us. My wife and I are so blessed and feel so good that we called out His name in the hour of trials, tests, and tribulations for the LORD dwells in the praises of His people.

ROMANS 8: 31 goes on to say:

"What then shall we say in response to this? If God is for us who can be against us? He who did not spare his own son, but gave him for us all- how will he not also a long with him, graciously give us all things? Who will bring any charge against those whom God has chosen? It is God who justifies. Who is he that condemns? Christ Jesus who died- more than that, who was raised to life is at the right hand side of God and is also interceding for us. Who shall separate us from the love of Christ? Shall trouble or hardship or persecution or famine or nakedness or danger or sword? As it is written:

For your sake we face death all day long; we are considered as sheep to be slaughtered. No, in all things we are more than conquerors, through him who loved us. For I am convinced that neither death nor life, neither angels nor demons, neither height nor depth, nor anything else in all creation will be able to separate us from the love of God that is in Jesus Christ our LORD."

If God is on our side, no one, then, can be against us. No one can accuse, judge, criticize, or condemn us because Jesus Christ, our mediator, attorney, and intercessor, is justifying us before the Father. We are reconciled to God and we are more than conquerors. Surely, no weapons formed against us, by the enemy, shall prosper; and nothing can separate us from the love of our God through Christ Jesus who died for us. No suffering, no hardship, no pain, no struggle, no deprivation or lack, no war, danger or even starvation can separate us from the love of God. The devil is a liar and a murderer as he is described in,

JOHN 8:44

"You belong to your father, the devil, and you want to carry out your father's desires. He was a murderer from the beginning, not holding the truth, for there is no truth in him. When he lies he speaks his native language, for he is a liar and the father of lies."

You read Satan's ministry, mission, and vision in JOHN 10:10 that he only comes, but to steal, kill, and destroy. The devil is a "father" and has children too. This is what Jesus Christ said, that, those who are willing vessels to do wickedness and evil are the devil's children and they are simply carrying out their father's desires. The devil's evil nature is not only in actively being involved in sin, but he is a murderer. That is his original nature. His native language is telling lies. That is his basic original first mother tongue. Remember, on the contrary, Jesus is full of truth and grace. He is the light, the life, the way, and absolute truth. He came so that we could have life, and have it in abundance. The opposite is true of the devil; he is the darkness, the killer, deceiver, liar, and accuser of brethren. He has strategies and scheme as the major opposition party against the legitimate theocratic, divine government of God our legitimate and rightful Father-God.

## THE DEVIL'S EVIL STRATEGY

The devil sneaks in subtly and swiftly in our lives, situations, circumstances, trials, tests,tribulations,events, and afflictions and uses them as weapons through our thoughts, words, and actions. This way, he ultimately uses us as vessels, conduits, tools, and transmissions of evil and wickedness. He jumps in to use our hardships, misfortunes, troubles, problems, persecutions and moments of discouragement to infuse doubt in the goodness of our God and tells the lie that we are left all alone. He uses lies and deception to derail us from the tracks that lead us to the fulfillment of our God-given purposes, missions, visions, and destinies. Sadly, this is how the devil uses such moments of our lives as weapons to work destruction in us. It is in such moments that he influences us to do acts of transgression, sin, and iniquity as he takes advantage of our weak moments and desperations. He uses manipulation by causing us to feel guilty and uses fear to paralyze us. These are the devil's weapons of mass destruction to many.

In order for us to defeat him we should use the weapon of prayer to counteract his attacks on our lives. We need to pray effective prayers of warfare and invoke God to fight on our behalf in the spiritual realm. We must decree positive declarations and speak God's written word and say: "No weapons formed, forged, or fashioned against us shall prosper in Jesus' name! we must plead the blood of Jesus on our situations and proclaim that we are more than conquerors through Jesus who loves and protects us from the devil's onslaughts. We should decree and declare that the devil is a bold face, big mouth liar and we should refuse his tactics of intimidation. The devil is a murderer, he is the ancient serpent of old whose head was crushed by our LORD, King, Master, and savior, Jesus Christ the son of God. This way, God fights for us through our faith and words of our mouths. God, then casts down the devil's schemes, plans projects against our lives and breaks all his evil intentions and ideas.

At the core of his nature and being are lies, deceptions, wicked imaginations and outright evil. He is a braggadocios, schizophrenic, megalomania and pompaliceited marodius. He seeks to devour us! He desires to steal our stuff! He wants to kill us!

He aims at utterly destroying us. He basically wants to separate us from our God and take us out at any chance he gets. He is so determined and unrelenting, not letting up, or giving up so easily. He is a ruthless predator who preys and feeds on God's children. Jesus Christ is the lion of Judah, but the devil is also like a roaring lion seeking who to devour. While God is the Father of truth, grace, and all creation, the devil is the father of lies, legalism, deception, and destruction. He is a thief and destroyer. We need to choose who is our father and legitimate authority over our lives between the devil and God. The Holy bible says in the book of 2 CORINTHIANS 10: 3-

"For though we live in the world, we do not wage war as the world does. The weapons we fight with are not the weapons of the world. On the contrary, they have divine power to demolish strongholds. We demolish arguments and every pretension that sets itself up against the knowledge of God, and take captive every thought to make it obedient to Christ. And we will be ready to punish every act of disobedience, once your obedience is complete."

This is this how we fight in self defense against our mortal enemy in defiance against his wicked suggestions and insinuations. He is not our ally, neither is he on our side, he is our enemy and does not need to be given any foothold or chance to step into our lives which are sacred territory. We need to fight with every ounce of spiritual energy we have in us before he can topple us completely and subdue us. We need to remain vigilant and alert because Jesus Christ gave us the victory against the wiles and viles of the enemy."

REVELATIONS 12:7 speaks of the devil in this account of the attempted coup de tat against God in Heaven and how he was defeated and cast out to this earth where he continues to wreck havoc on our lives as the children of God.

"And there was war in heaven, Michael and his angels fought the dragon, and the dragon and his angels fought back. But he was not strong enough, and they lost their place in heaven. The great dragon was hurled down-that ancient serpent called the devil or satan, who leads the world astray, he was hurled down on the earth, and his angels with him. Then I heard a loud voice in heaven say:

"Now have come the salvation and the power and Kingdom of God, and the authority of his Christ, for the accuser of our brothers, who accuses them before God day and night, has been hurled down. They overcame him by the blood of the Lamb and by the word of their testimony; they did not love their lives as to shrink from death. Therefore rejoice you heavens and you who dwell in them! But woe to the earth and the sea, because the devil has gone down to you! He is filled with fury, because he knows that his time is short."

When the dragon saw that he had been hurled to the earth, he pursued the woman who had given birth to the male child." When we skip and go to verse 17, the Holy Bible concludes this chapter by saying:

"Then the dragon was enraged at the woman and went off to make war against the rest of her offspring-those who obey God's commandments and hold to the testimony of Jesus."

The Christian walk and testimony of Jesus by the children of God, enrages and infiltrates the dragon, the ancient serpent, Satan the devil. He comes after us with nothing less than his key mission, which is to steal, kill, and destroy us according to the confirmation made by the above account of his intentions and aims. Once you decide and resolve to follow Jesus Christ, be sure that the devil will come after you with all the venom and vengeance he has against the children of God. He will come after you with all that he has in his book of wickedness, ruthlessness, and evil. But always remember that we have a defender, the boy child, Emmanuel, Jesus the Christ our savior and Messiah.

Do not forget that God is with us always and all the way up to the end of the age. Jesus Christ conquered death and all the temptations, tests and attacks of the enemy. He rose out of the grave and defeated death. He is our resurrected King. He is alive, and he is seated at the right hand side of the Father defending us against the accusations of the evil one. He is our savior whose blood cries out to the Father on our behalf saying: "Mercy! Mercy! Mercy! Before the mercy seat of our Father in Heaven. This is how he defends us and continually pleads our case in intercession before the Father of lights and refutes all the legalistic arguments and accusations made against us by the accuser of the brethren, the devil, our arch-enemy.

God's grace is more than sufficient for us at all times. God the father looks at His son's blood and sees us the flawless righteousness of God. By this token, the accuser is rendered ineffective because of the power of the blood and the name of the slain Lamb of God, Jesus the Christ. By His blood, we are victorious, as seen in the evidence of our car crush testimony. As you have read, Job was one of Satan's victims of his relentless accusations, torments, and attacks. Many Apostles and Prophets were slain because of this raging war between good and evil. Our King paid the price and ransom for the atonement of our sins and set us free from all bondage and captivity. Our sins were washed away by His sacred blood on the cross and intersection of the road of human history.

Though this tragic car accident we were involved in may have been intended to break and destroy us, our God protected us and turned it for his glory. The evil one may have intended and expected us (my wife and I) to blame and accuse each other, or even complain that, I, the driver did not exercise the necessary and enough caution; hence exposing and subjecting my wife and baby to potential danger and even probable death.

More especially these two beautiful lives; of my wife and daughter, who both possibly had long productive lives ahead of them. Just imagine the gravity and magnitude of the matter where my young beautiful wife broke her spine and could have been paralyzed for life, and the possibility of suffering a stroke during the surgery, let alone the probability of being bound to a wheel chair for the rest of her life. She probably could have suffered this fate. How sad and unfortunate could that have been? Other possibilities could have been fatal injuries like broken limbs- legs or arms and rendering us immobile and taking away our self dependence and subjecting us to assisted living? What a tragedy!

"Then the dragon was enraged at the woman and went off to make war against the rest of her offspring, those who obey God's commandments and hold on to the testimony of Jesus." This particular verse tells it all that the devil is at war with us and means business to do us harm- to steal our stuff, kill us, and destroy us and the things that belong to us. He is very serious because he is running out of time before he is going to be thrown in hell, the lake of fire that has been prepare for him, his angels-the demons, and those who have chosen to follow him. We have some critical decisions and choices to make as to who is our father and as to who controls our lives.

These are the strategies that the devil had intended to achieve through our car accident, but he failed lamentably because my wife and I had the right perspective of seeing God's hand in our plight instead of blaming or accusing each other as the devil uses each and every negative opportunity to blame and accuse. These should have been the sure symptoms that could have proved that the devil was in operation in such instances as in the event of our car accident. In the aftermath, a lot of negative talk could have ensued, but glory to God, nothing of that sort ever happened. No guilt or shame. We simply thanked God for saving us and took good care of each other with positive words of encouragement.

The devil's motives are clearly to break apart, break up, and break down relationships by taking advantage of any opportunity he gets. As it has already been shown and proved in the Bible accounts of how he broke the first relationship between God and Adam and Eve. He separated God from his own children- the human race, alienating God from His own wonderful creation through the strategy of division, disunity, and fragmentation. The devil destroyed and broke in pieces the relationship God had with the man and woman He had created through the sin of deception resulting in disobedience, and ultimately death and the impending hell for the devil, his demons, and those who chose to obey and follow him. This is evidence of how the devil is after the offspring of the woman- humanity.

ROMANS 5:12

"Therefore, just as sin entered the world through one man, and death through sin, and in this way death came to all people, because all sinned-for before the law was given, sin was in the world. But sin is not taken into account when there is no law. Nevertheless, death reigned from the time of Adam to the time of Moses, even over those who did not sin by breaking a command, as did Adam, who was a pattern of the one to come.

But the gift is not like the trespass. For if the many died by the trespass of the one man, how much more did God's grace and the gift that came by the grace of the one man, Jesus Christ, overflow to the many! Again, the gift of God is not like the result of the one man's sin: The judgment followed one sin and brought condemnation, but the gift followed many trespasses and brought justification. For if by the trespass of one man, death reigned through that one man, how much more will those who receive God's abundant provision of grace and the gift of righteousness reign in life through the one man, Jesus Christ.

Consequently, just as the result of one trespass was the condemnation for all men, so also the result the one act of righteousness was justification that brings life for all men. For just as through the disobedience of one man the many were made sinners, also through the obedience of the one man the many will be made righteous.

The law was added so that trespass might increase. But where sin increased, grace increased all the more, so that just as sin reigned in death, so also grace might reign through righteousness to bring eternal life through Jesus Christ our Lord."

The devil's strategy of fragmentation shows itself through the acts of fault-finding, unnecessary arguments and disagreements causing unresolved conflicts, criticism, judgment, self-justification, condemnation, and acts of legalism. Once these things happening between and among people, you know that the devil is at work because these series of actions cause reactions whereby the one person attacked will develop a defense mechanism of countering and counteracting. This becomes a whole process and exchange of incrimination and recrimination. This was very evident when Adam and Eve where being asked by God why they had chosen to disobey Him. Adam blamed and accused Eve and Eve blamed it all on the serpent. This is what happens when the devil infuses confusion in a situation.

When the Holy Bible says we all became sinners because of the sin of one man, a lot of questions must have started running through your mind asking a lot of questions as to what sin, you, as an individual have committed. The analogue I can use to expain this is; when a parent of a lineage or geneology that has a gene of cancer or some other terminal or genetic disease that runs though the blood and genes of a paricular family tree, becomes an inherited disease passed down by forefathers from generation to generation down to the offspring, what genetic composition will have caused this perpetution of a genetic defect or disorder that runs through the blood and genes of a certain or particular family? This is the same inherited sin nature that the human race inherited from Adam and Eve. Subquently, the grace and righteousness through the blood of Jesus Christ that was shed on Calvary took away and removed the curse of sin and cured all the ills of humanity's fall from God's grace.

When these vices of blame games manifest, the devil has spewed and injected his venom in a relationship. Consequently, this causes emotional turmoil and hurt that begins to surface through physical manifestations.- our hormones discharge an inbalance in our body fluids, causing physical manifetations like headache and even depression through stress and causing social, spiritual, and moral separation. Legalism nullifies and refutes grace;

where right and wrtong reigns, as opposed to unconditional love and forgiveness, there is disunity, division, and fragmentation of social and spiritual cohesion resulting in manifestations of egocentric tendencies and self-centeredness. When grace reigns, there is unconditional love, understanding, mercy, forgiveness, compassion, empathy, sympathy, kindness, peace, concord and living in one accord. The absence of grace breeds discord, disrespect, rebellion, disobedience and unforgivess. Whreas blame and accusation potentially produce: anger, resentment, bitterness, self-pity, poor self-image, and low self-esteem, lack of self control, and ultimately, communication breaks down and the relationship in question suffers.

Through all this ordeal, the life and death lessons we learnt are that, what the devil might have meant for evil, but God turned it all for good. While the devil intended to instil fear, morbidity, and cripple us, but God gave us what my friend in New York, Pastor Dale Gurajena of Fortress of Faith Tabernacle calls stubborn faith, which in my own words is radical, relentless, and unflinching fearlessness. My wife demonstrated this kind of faith and fearlessness. After being discharged from Hospital, she was immediately on the go doing even more than what she was doing before she was injured. One would have expected her to slow down because she was hurting from the fatal C2 spine injury.

We refused to be intimidated, slowed down, or rendered morbid. One would have expected to see us timid and immobile. We resolved to go on the move. We made a decision to make no deals, no concessions, no negotiations, no begging or pleading, or even asking for our freedom from our enemy the devil. We demanded our freedom and reserved our deliverance from our captor, oppressor, suppressor, depressor, intimidator, and exterminator who is also an eliminator, the devil whose sole aim was to destroy us. He failed to hold us down in his many forms of captivity and bondage which he does to his victims, but instead he set us on a process of radical divine spiritual metamorphosis. He wanted to use evil tactics by taking advantage of our injuries, material deprivation- the loss of our car and earning money by not letting us to go to work.

God's providence and provision came through Papa Florian Kamanda of RICC who continued to pay us for ministry work in spite of my absence from work at the church. We thank him for being a willing conduit of God's provision. Indeed, we thank God for using him and some of our friends who supported us financially during this difficult time. God, once again, proved that He is Jehovah Jireh, our Provider who used these willing vessels to transmit and deliver his provision, blessing, and support during these tough times. The devil's evil and wicked intentions were defeated once again. We emerged victorious and triumphant. We did not request but demanded our release and freedom from the dungeon of the dragon. This was a: "Give it, or else situation." This means that if this situation required aggressive action or violent behavior for us to break loose and be free, we just did it without his permission, delay, or prolonged procrastination, or even hesitation. We did not sympathize with the evil plottings of our enemy.

We just had to get our freedom through our Master, Lord, and King, Jesus Christ who set us free. Just as the Holy Bible says in the book of JOHN 18:36 "So if the son sets you free, you will be free indeed." NIV. Our creator defended us at whatever cost.

Our daily struggles through trials, tribulations, and tragedies help to build and form us, transforming us to a level of transcending our limitations and causing us to come out stronger, wiser, and keeping us going through all the inevitable constant changes of Life's-radical spiritual metamorphosis. The question is: "Can we continue to be grateful for the calamities and tragedies we go through?" and the answer is, yes, firstly, because they help us answer the most important and fundamental questions of our existence. The basic knowledge is that we did not create ourselves. We were created by a supernatural spiritual being we call by many names, but whom I call God. I need this basic knowledge because I am fashioned, made, and formed as the most sophisticated and mysteriously complex being. The human body is the most complex and mysterious work of engineering that no one else can make but God.

Secondly, God did not waste His time, effort and energy for nothing when He made the Human machine- the body and the life He put in it. He definitely had a divine purpose. This teaches us to love our origins and source of our very nature and being. It also brings us to the realization that we are interconnected and interdependent on all that is created in the universe within which we exist and live. We come to appreciate, thank, and be grateful for the privilege of life and living as related to our creator who is the very sole source of our lives and being. We begin to love Him and in return love ourselves and others and all other things in the universe and entire creation including our common struggles, troubles and problems as we seek solutions. As we realize that we were not placed here on this earth by accident causes as to know that there are solutions to all our problems that come from a loving and caring creator, our God. With this knowledge, we begin to look beyond our imperfections, shortcomings, flaws, and weaknesses. We stop being the judge of what is not right with ourselves or somebody else and know that God is able to take care of all our problems and concerns and inadequacies. When we love our creator, ourselves, and others, we develop a healthy sense of self image and self esteem. We abandon the poor perceptions created by inferiority complex that we should live to impress somebody else apart from our creator.

We become firmly and solidly grounded on our beliefs and faith of who created us and for what purpose he created us. We are deeply rooted in the truth from which we grow and bear fruit by living a life of purpose and fulfillment and forsake and abandon the perceptions of poor self image, low self esteem which are all rooted in inferiority and/ or superiority complexes. We are all of the same equal value in the eyes of our creator. We were created to accomplish an important purpose; so nothing will deter or stop that purpose apart from ourselves. God will orchestrate and command the universe and all that is in it to position you to achieve your God-given assignment on this earth before you can go back to him to give an account before Him who made you.

Therefore, look deep and beyond the natural and superficial and be connected to the divine, spiritual, and supernatural. Look beyond the mistakes, flaws, and weaknesses of others and yourself and know that there is a God who will push and see you through all your calamities, tragedies, trials, tests, and tribulations because they form us and transform us and raise us to higher ground as they help us to know there is a God who cares and looks out for us. When he solves our natural day to day problems and struggles, we have a reason to be grateful and thankful that there is a higher being, who is not only conscious and alive, but cares, and knows enough of our inability, lack, and insufficiencies in grappling, handling and solving all the problems and issues we encounter in our lives. Our struggles and problems raise us to heights we would otherwise have never reached had we not experienced them. Our challenges challenge us enough to higher heights and reach our innate potential that can sometimes be activated by the problems we face and catapult us to progress and go towards a trajectory and direction that our maker drives us to go, reach and achieve our purpose as originally intended by Him. This might mean material dispossession, deprivation, loss, lack, and even tragedy as the car accident we were involved in and took me to a divine encounter; without which, this spiritual and supernatural experience could not have happened though it came with a high and terrible cost. This event can't have a price tag attached to it and its value traded for nothing.

In this life we will meet opposition, resistance, troubles, hardships, and all forms of sufferings in order for us to get tested and tried in the divine fire of God's refining furnace. Think of the magnitude of the test of our faith even to face a death experience like what happened to me and my wife and still be brought out by our God who gives and takes away life. All glory be to such a wonderful God! He will never leave us alone nor forsake us, because, He who is in us is far much greater than he who is in the world- our adversary and arch-enemy- the evil devil and his wicked and devilish demons possessed by his spirit of pride, hate, and destruction towards God's children and His creation. Our God has assured us that, despite all this, He will continue to be with us until the end of the age when all will pass away but His word remains true to the last letter and dot. We will always come out and emerge even more than conquerors and victorious as we breakthrough all the barricades, detours, booby traps, obstructions, and stumbling blocks thrown our way as we tread through the roads of our lives. We were not just created and abandoned on this earth to fend and fight for ourselves, but we have a loving Father who loves, cares and fights our battles in spite of whatever wars and woes we face in our lives' rough and tough roads as we journey through this earth and lives. He knows each one of us, He cares, loves, trains, teaches, protects, and prepares us for good and great works ahead of us. Our troubles are not for nothing. They are not intended to torture and torment us, they have a divine meaning when you search and look deeper and beyond the superficial and shallow surface of things. Do not dwell on the trivial, insignificant, and irrelevant issues of life's happenings; look deeper within and you will find the meaning in all things; good or bad, negative or positive, just remember that "all things work for the good of those who love God and have been called according to His purpose." We have been called to believe with hope. We need to persevere and endure all the challenges we meet along the highways and by-ways of the paths and roads of our lives. We are not alone, neither are we neglected by our creator. We need to face life's challenges with an attitude of thanksgiving, gratitude, worship, and praise to the most high God who knows everything we are going through. He is all powerful and present in our lives at all times in all situations, events, and circumstances.

We are not left alone in this universe, He is with us. That is why His name is Emmanuel which means God is with us. This should be a blessed assurance, encouragement, and comfort that should strengthen you when you feel left all alone, helpless, and hopeless. There is hope! Help is right there with you and you just need to call upon His name because it is not a myth or illusion that Jesus is alive and came to rescue you out of your troubles and concerns. He cared for you enough to come down from heaven and take the human form and died for you.

He came to deliver the good news that God is with us and that He loves and has forgiven us our sins through the shedding of blood on the cross of Calvary, His death, burial and resurrection. This is the blessed assurance of the signs, miracles, and wonders of a living and loving God, who came on this earth to live, suffer and face all our human troubles and emerged victorious, even through conquering death through His resurrection, giving us hope that suffering and death are not the end of this life. There is eternal life! We must just believe, receive the gift of grace and have faith in Him who came to die for and assured us that He will be with us always through it all. This is the faith that raised us from our death.

# CHAPTER SEVEN

ROMANS 5:3 says: "Not only so, but we also rejoice in our sufferings, because we know that suffering produces perseverance, perseverance, character; and character, hope. And hope does not disappoint us, because God has poured out into our hearts the Holy Spirit, whom he has given us.

You see, at just the right time, when we were still powerless, Christ died for the ungodly." Verse 8 of the same says: "But God demonstrated his own love for us in this: while we were still sinners, Christ died for us." Further down to verse 11, the matter is concluded that: "Not only is this so, but we also rejoice in God through our Lord Jesus Christ, through whom we have now received reconciliation." This is the core of the good news also called the gospel that we are forgiven and reconciled to our Father God through Jesus Christ our redeemer. Once we believe in Him and confess His name, we are saved. We need to share this good news and that is the sole purpose of this book.

Remember also that we need to have God at the very core of our being, physical, and spiritual DNA so that the information, knowledge and data enshrined, inscripted, embedded, and engraved in us, engulfs, and infiltrates our whole very being; take root and find residence and a permanent dwelling place within us. You have heard these words spoken over and over and have now become a cliché:

"Junk in, junk out! And adding to this, I say: "God in, God out!, Jesus in, Jesus out, faith in, faith out, prayer in, prayer out, praise in, praise out, worship in, worship out, and also the opposite is true that: devil in, devil out, demon in, demon out!" So, the important question that remains for us to answer is: "What are we putting in our system which forms our DNA and "spiritual software?"

Do not forget, but remember also what the Holy Bible says in the book of MARK 12:29

"The most important one," answered Jesus, "is this; Hear O Israel, the Lord our God, the Lord is one. Love the Lord your God with all your heart and with all your Soul and with all your mind, and with all your strength. The second is this: Love your neighbor as yourself. There is no commandment greater than these."

This is the whole reason why I said, by me declaring and proclaiming that, "Jesus is alive!" and on the other hand, my wife saying: "Thank you Jesus!" in our dying moments means that our "spiritual softwares" are full of nothing but faith in God through our Lord Jesus Christ. Our souls and spirits are full of worship and praise. We are always thanking and praising Him in all situations even in the least expected circumstances like our tragic car accident. We praised and worshipped Him by saying these words of thanks and praises in our unconscious states and in the most unfortunate moments of tragedy and calamity proving that we are saved by His grace.

All this experience and our declarations meant that we are filled with, and full of what we fed our hearts minds, souls, spirits, and inner beings. We can say that we are full of nothing but glorification of the name of Jesus Christ our Lord, Master, and king. All this goes to prove and show that He rules our beings as confessed by our mouths and the words we spoke and came through our physical hardware. All this came through the words of our lips, mouths and tongues. This is our core confession. This brings us to what I call the seven "R's" of Jesus Christ's Ministry.

1. REPENTANCCE: These are the very first words He spoke when preached at the very beginning of His ministry. These are the same words spoken by John the Baptist in the wilderness. This is a very important call that demands the need to continually repent of our sins every day. The Holy Bible says, we have all fallen short of the glory of God and we have all sinned. It also says anyone who says they have not sinned are calling God a liar. The Bible declares that let all men lie and only be true. Therefore, we all need to admit of our sinful nature and repent. This is the crossroads and turning point that we all need to make the right decision when confronted with these questions and choices to make.

   MATTHEW 4:17 From that time on Jesus began to preach, "repent for the Kingdom of heaven is near."

   MATTHEW 3:1-2 also says:

   "In those days John the Baptist came, preaching in the desert of Judea and saying; "Repent, for the Kingdom of heaven is near."

2. RECONCILIATION: After admitting our sins we need to seek reconciliation. There is an old Hymn that says: "What can take away my sins? Nothing but the blood of Jesus. For us to be reconciled to God our Father we need to call upon the name of Jesus whose blood washed away our sins on the cross of Golgotha where He was crucified and died for us. We received the forgiveness of our sins through the shedding of the blood of the lamb of God Jesus Christ. Through the pouring of His blood on the cross we became the righteousness of God. We are now reconnected and rejoined back to our God, our creator. 2CORINTHIANS 5:8 says:

   "All this is from God, who reconciled us to Himself through Christ and gave us the ministry of reconciliation: that God was reconciling the world to himself in Christ, not counting people's sins against them. And he has committed to us the message of reconciliation. We are therefore Christ's ambassadors, as though Christ was making his appeal through us, we implore you on Christ's behalf: Be reconciled to God. God made him who had no sin to be sin for us, so that in him we might become the righteousness of God. His blood is the means of propitiation by which the righteousness of Jesus becomes our righteousness in God's sight." When we read ISAIAH 61:1, this very message is confirmed.

"The Spirit of the Sovereign LORD is upon me, because the LORD has anointed me to preach good news to the poor. He has sent me to bind up the brokenhearted, to proclaim freedom for the captives and release from darkness for the prisoners, to proclaim the year of the LORD's favor and the day of vengeance of our God, to comfort all who mourn, and provide for those who grieve in Zion- to bestow on them the crown of beauty instead of ashes, the oil of gladness instead of mourning, and a garment of praise instead of a spirit of despair. They will be called Oaks of righteousness, a planting of the LORD for the display of his spleandor.They will rebuild the ancient ruins and restore the places long devastated; they will renew the ruined cities that have been devastated for generations."

This is a message of hope from despair and hopelessness. This takes me to the next "R."

3. REPARATION: The death of Jesus christ, the shedding of His blood, resurrection, and ascension to heaven repaired the broken relationship between God the Father and humanity. God was separated from his children-the human race for many generations from the time of Adam's sin of disobedience to the time of Christ's obedience which repaired the ancient damage and ruins.

JOHN 3:16 says:

"For God so loved the world that he gave his one and only son that whoever believes in him shall not perish but have eternal life. For God did not send his son into the world to condemn the world, but to save the world through him. Whoever believes in him is not condemned, but whoever does not believe stands condemned already because he has not believed in the name of God's one and only son. This is the verdict: Light has come into the world, but men loved darkness instead of light because their deeds were evil. Everyone who does evil hates the light, and will not come into the light for fear that his deeds will be exposed. But whoever lives by the truth comes into the light, so that it may be seen plainly that what he has done has been done through God."

4. RECLAIMING:

Jesus Christ's mission on this earth was to reclaim us from the grip of the devil and take us back to himself from the damnation of hell to eternal life and have life in Heaven with him forever. Heaven is our rightful inheritance and destination when we go away from this earth. Heaven is our royal abode, and not hell. We are his treasure that he took back to himself through the shedding of his blood, and the hope of eternal life through His resurrection.

5. RESTITUTION: Jesus Christ paid the ultimate price through His agonizing suffering and death on the cross. He ransomed us from eternal condemnation and death. He paid it all for us on the cross of Calvary on the hill of Golgotha and gave us eternal life. What a ransom to pay? This is much more than we deserved. This is unmerited favor! His grace is more than sufficient for us and He is worthy to be worshipped and praised with hearts of gratitude and thanksgiving for taking all the curses, judgement, sin, and death we were supposed to suffer and pay for.

6. RESTORATION: The ultimate purpose of Jesus Christ's Ministry was to restore us to our original place and position in all creation and to be reconnected and reconciled to our Father so that the dominion, power, and authroity given to us at creation is restored to us.

Now we have the right to our eternal sacred inheritance to rule over all creation with Christ our LORD. Everything that the devil had stolen from us has been given back in full through restoration of the work that was done by Christ Jesus our Master. The process of restoration was done through His coming down to earth and take upon the form of man and got wrapped up in flesh on this earthly realm as Emmanuel whose literal meaning is God is with us reconciling us to God our Father and restoring a broken relationship between our creator and us.

7. RETURNING: Jesus Christ is coming back again to take us where He is; as it is written in JOHN 14:1 which says:

"Do not let your hearts be troubled. Trust in God; trust also in me. In my Father's house are many rooms; if it were not so, I would have told you, I am going to prepare a place for you. And if I go to prepare a place for you, I will come back and take you with me that you also may be where I am. You know the way to the place where I am going."

Thomas said to him, "LORD, we don't know where you are going, so how can we know the way?"

Jesus answered, "I am the way, and the truth and the life. No one comes to the Father except through me, If you really knew me, you would know my Father as well. From now on, you do know him and have seen him."

ACTS 1:10

"They were looking intently up into the sky as he was going, when suddenly two men dressed in white stood beside them. "Men of Galilee." They said. "Why do you stand here looking into the sky? This same Jesus, who has been taken from you into heaven, will come back in the same way you have seen him go into heaven."

Jesus said He would be with us always up to the end of the age in MATTEW 28:20 "And surely I am with you always, to the very end of the age." This is very comforting to know that we are not alone. We have our solace in Emmanuel, who is God and is always with us to the very end of the age until he returns. These words are confirmed in the most popular Psalm written by David through all the ages which is found in

PSALM 23: 1

"The LORD is my shepherd, I shall not be in want; he makes me lie down in green pastures, he leads me beside quiet waters, he restores my soul. He guides me in paths of righteousness for his name's sake. Even though I walk through the valley of the shadow of death, I will fear no evil, for you are with me, your rod and your staff, they comfort me.

You prepare a table before me in the presence of my enemies, you anoint my head with oil, my cup overflows, surely goodness and love will follow me all the days of my life, and I will dwell in the house of the LORd forever."

The irony and paradox of this verse or poem written by David long ago while he was tending his father's animals in the green pastures and brooks, it actually came to pass in many instances of his life. It came to fulfillment when David fought and killed Goliath in the valley of Ellah. David actually walked through the real physical valley of death and feared no evil for God was with him.

Indeed, Goliath stood as a symbol of fear and death. He threatened the armies of Israel and they dreaded him. The army generals and King Saul, all trembled in their boots when he threatened them to kill the man who would challenge him. When David stood against him to take the challenge.

The giant threatened to kill David and feed his flesh to the birds of the air of the sky. In that real life experience David did walk physically in the valley of the shadow of death with faith and praise, and ultimately slew Goliath for God was with him.

It is true that the power of life and death is in the tongue, as the Holy Bible says, and David triumphed over Goliath and death in the valley of death. And God did prepare a table before David in the presence of his enemies; the LORD was his shepherd. This young boy stands as an encouragement for all ages in all situations of life that stand before us as fierce giants threatening us. We should never be intimidated by these evil giants found in our sufferings, toubles, trials, and tribulations.

Similarly, my wife and I walked through the valley of the shadow of death and we also feared no eveil for God was with us. Surely, God's goodness, love, and mercy, followed us all the days of our lives, and always will according to God's promises in His word. Our God is good and great. He rescued us out of the terrible car accident which was the valley of the shadow of our would- be-death. By reading this scripture of Psalm 23, which came alive to us through this car accident experience, you can tell that David had the Holy Spirit in him and could accurately foretell and speak of what was to come even in his real experiences.

David was not only a great warrior but also a true Prophet through whom God spoke and predicted events of the future. These deep insights revealed to him go to confirm that God divinely inspired him to speak of things that were to come in the future tied to his destiny.

According to this, I drew a conclusion that destiny is not an occurance of chance that happens by accident, but it is a divinely motivated purpose and chain of events that happen in a series of well calculated experiences that prepare the individual to fulfill that purpose. God is the one that forms, makes, orchestrates these events in an individual's life who was created with the appropriate and specific propensities and personality traits, qualities, abilities, aptitudes, capacities, gifts,and talents formulated and designed to undertake and accomplish the specific divine purpose in a given life span, life time, geographical location and season already preordained and predestined.

These special and unique personality traits are only perculiar to a particular individual equipped to fulfill the mission of God's intentional and deliberate vision and dream. This particular individual is endowed and entrusted with natural and divine or spiritual traits with required intellectual faculties, temperament and voliton. This individual possesses a divinely inherent passion to embark on this personal journey that only God sets them on.

They are divinely moulded, and well designed in every aspect: physically, emotionally, spiritually, socially, and intellectually. They are also positioned in a particular geographical location in order to experience well orchestrated series of events, situations, circumstances, and experiences that translate into a plan of action well executed by the supreme spiritual divine being-God who already preordained and predestined everything. He is the all- knowing God, the omniscient one who inspires, guides, and directs the individual in order to fulfill the calling.

David, inspired by the Spirit of God wrote the PSALM 139:16 which says:

"Your eyes saw my unformed body. All the days ordained for me were written in your book before one of them came to be."

This is an extremely profound insightful statement which agrees and tallies with JEREMIAH 1:5 which goes on to say:

"Before I formed you in the womb I knew you, before you were born I set you apart; and appointed you as a prophet to the nations."

Just as God spoke to Jeremiah that He knew him before he was formed and even before he was born and set him apart for a specific purpose; equally, each one of us is like that and the same in the eyes of God who created us and assigned a purpose to every one a specific task, we just have to know what our calling, purpose, and assignment is on this earth and immediately embark on it.

However, there is no promise or guarantee that everything is going to be easy as each one of us walks along the various journeys of our lives. It can be very tough and precarious as proved by the life histories, personal stories, and life experiences of all those that went ahead before us. Those that walked with God like: Abraham, Moses, Job, Joseph, David, Jesus Christ the son of God, Peter, Paul, Stephen, to mention, but a few. They all had their own shares of trials and tribulations; so do we also expect going through our own troubles as we meet many problems along the way.

For instance, let's look at david's life from the time he was anointed by the prophet Samuel, up to his coronation as the King of Israel. He went through a time of testing, trials and tribulations in order to form in him the required character for his future divine role. He went through hardship, suffering, calamities, troubles and tragedies, but he depended entirely on God, and God alone through all of it. Hence, David is the only man said to be after God's own heart.

A lot of questions still linger around his life and legacy. Did he make mistakes? Did he have character flaws and weaknesses? Was he perfect and did everything right before God and man? Was he a holy man? Did he do some wrong things? The answer is: No, not perfect, he was a sinner with flaws just like anybody else. Nevertheless, he is still called the man after God's won heart up to this day. David still towers tall in the annals of history as a legendary hero. Do you know why? It's all by God's grace.

Even though he was fallible, he always cried out to God in repentance each time he did something wrong. He was an ordinary sinner just like anybody else. What distinguished him is a heart of repentance which earned him God's mercy and unmerited favor among his contemporaries. He stands out as the greatest King of Israel because he set the precedent and example of a heart of true repentance as he focused on God alone.

Despite this, did he have it easy? Did he get kingship on a silver plate? David never had it easy. His life was not a walk in the park as he strove on his way towards the crown and the palace. He endured harship and persevered. He did not walk or sleep on a road of roses. He persisted against the tide of resistance and opposition and kept his heart on God alone.

His flame of fire and burning passion to forge ahead against all odds was not extinguished by any waters of discouragement but fanned by the winds of divine destiny and purpose as he pushed against the tide of persecution, failure, and shame. He pushed against the mighty waves of resistance and war until he became King and left an enduring legacy that even history cannot deny or erase. That is what ROMANS 5:3 means when it says:

"Not only so, but we also rejoice in our sufferings, because we know that suffering produces perseverance, perseverance, character, and character, hope. And hope does not diappoint us, because God poured out his love into our hearts by the Holy Spirit whom he has given us.

David went through all of this. You and I are no exception to these negative experiences of life. If you and I go through any of these experiences of life, we do not need to have a victim mentality. We are not the first, nor are we the last to experience such, neither has this began happening today. It has been happening for many ages and still happening today and will continue to happen even tomorrow; we must always remember that we are not alone through it all. God is with us all the time.

You have now shared my story and you must know that it can happen to any one, any time, anywhere. It is a part of this life we are living in this physical earthly realm. This word and stories of long ago and today, do still confirm that, through all of this, and in spite of all adversity, we can still prevail and fulfill God's divine purposes in our own lives with all our flaws, imperfections, faults, weaknesses, mistakes, and wrongs. The greatest benefit of all this is that we must learn lessons from all these experiences whether positive or negative. We must repent when we are wrong and change like David. All these experiences of our lives are transfromative forces.

What can separate us from the love of God our creator? Is it our sins, iniquities, transgressions or sufferings? The resolve is: nothing can separate us from the love of our God. Nothing can even deter us from fulfilling his divinely inspired purposes and destinies. As you can see from many examples through the Bible stories and our own very life experiences. We are all subjected to our own fates and fortunes, and even sometimes blessings through our sufferings. We need to focus on God through everything we face in our lives.

It took a very long time, experiences, events, challenges, problems, choices, and actions for David to ascend to the throne. There is a throne and a crown made and prepared and waiting just for you and me. As we walk along this road, we might sometimes wear crowns of thorns, and not of gold and diamonds. You and I have heard and know that life happens. David's anointing happened in an instant, but it took a long time to materialize.

Instataneous gratification is like being born with a silver spoon in the mouth, but struggles are part of our growing up in strength, wisdom, maturity and stature. It is a process of preparation, equipping, and acquisitioning of the necessary knowledge and understanding so we can receive our blessings with a heart of gratitude. God has a good plan for each one of us and He knows your end before your beginning. He has counted and numbered your days already before anyone of them came to be. He knows the number of your hairs on your head. Is that not amazing? JEREMIAH 29:11 says: "For I know the plans I have for you," declares the LORD, "plans to prosper you and not to harm you, plans to give you a hope and a future." This confirms the Good plans that God has for us.

LUKE 12:7Jesus said: "Indeed, the very hairs of your head are all numbered. Don't be afraid; you are worthy more than many sparrows."

This tells us that God knows all the smallest and minutest details of our being. God cares for us, so we do not need to be afraid of the enemy who is always on the offensive attacking us. We have a defender and a protector who knows how to fight our battles and always wins.

1PETER 5:7 says: "Cast all your cares on him because he cares for you. Be self-controlled and alert. Your enemy the devil prowls around like a roaring Lion looking for someone to devour. Resist him, standing firm in the faith, because you know that your brothers throughout the world are undergoing the same kind of sufferings. And God of grace, who called you to his eternal glory in Christ, after you have suffered a little while, will himself restore you and make you strong, firm, and steadfast. To him be the power forever and ever.Amen.

This is the message of comfort and consolation that God is on our side. We might suffer for a little while, but God will always restore us and make us firm, strong, and steadfast. The Bible says in the book of LAMENTATIONS 3:22 "The steadfast love of the LORD never ceases; his mercies never come to an end; they are new every morning; great is your faithfulness" ESV. Our God is faithful and his mercies never come to and end. Each morning we wake up, we sure rest assured that God's mercies are new every morning.

# CHAPTER EIGHT

## THE LESSONS WE LEARNT THROUGH THIS EXPERIENCE:

The lessons we learnt through the experience of the car accident and the consequent fatal injuries we suferred are:

1. God exists beyond any shadow of a doubt. Our faith in God was solidified, and made firm by the suffering. God pieced up our broken pieces and glued them up with His mighty power. We had a kind of solidified faith as it is written in HEBREWS 11:1-6 which says: "Now faith is the substance of what we hope for and evidence of what is not seen." And verse 6 goes further to say: "Without faith, it is impossible to please God, because anyone who comes to him must believe that he exists and that he rewards those who earnestly seek him.

2. We were brought to a point where we learnt to love our God with all our hearts, all our minds, all our souls, and all our strength. This is the reciprocal love; as our relationship flows from Him to us, and from us to Him. This is the vertical nature of our reciprocal love relationship with Him.

3. We learnt to depend on God and God alone, first and foremost; then to love one and another. My wife and I shared a very caring relationship as we constantly checked on each other and asked how the other was feeling at any sound of a groan, sigh or unusual movement. We also learnt to love our friends and neighbors as we'd love

ourselves. The Golden rule became so real that it became so clear that we should do unto others as we'd have them do unto us- Loving God and His creation. Life proved to be so delicate, frail, and fragile and could be blown away like a puff of smoke or a cloud of dust at any time.

4. We learnt to worship God in good and bad times. This type of worship is what I call unconditional worship because it is not determined by events or happenings but by the spirit of true reverence to Him and just for who He is. This kind of worship is written in the book of JOHN 4:23-24 "Yet a time is

5. coming and has now come when the true worshipers will worship the Father in spirit and truth, for they are the kind of worshipers the father seeks. God is spirit and his worshipers must worship in spirit and in truth." Such is the kind of worship God is looking for. This kind of worship is not depent on favorable circumstances but worshiping Him at all times; praying unceasingly as it is written in the Book of 1THESSALONIANS 5:16 which says: "Be joyful always; pray continually; give thanks in all circumstances, for this is God's will for you in Christ Jesus." This entrenched in us an attitude of thanks and praises to Him in all situations and circumstances; glorifying and exalting His name as it is written in EPHESIANS 5:20 which says: "Always giving thanks to God the Father for everything, in the name of our LORD Jesus Christ.

6. We learnt to read and depend upon His word; to listen to it and act on it in faith. It became our daily bread and we learnt to meditate upon it day and night as it is written in the Book of JOSHUA 1:8 that says: "Do not let this Book of the law depart from your mouth; meditate on it day and night, so that you may be careful to do everything written in it. Then you will be prosperous and successful.

7. We learnt to be brave and courageous against terrifying circumstances as it is wriiten in JOSHUA 1:9 which reads: "Have I not commanded you? Be strong and courageous. Do not be terrified; do not be discouraged, for the LORD your God will be with you wherever you go. These words

are addressed to all who believe in God because what He spoke and did for others, He will do for all who put their trust in Him. 2 TIMOTHY 1:7 also reinforces these words and says: "For God did not give us a spirit of fear, but of power, of love and a sound mind."

8.   We learnt to continue to seek Him continually above everything else as it is written in MATTHEW 6:33 which reads as follows: "But seek first his Kingdom and his righteousness, and all these things will be given to you as well. Therefore do not worry about tomorrow, for tomorrow will worry about itself. Each day has enough trouble of its own.We began to let the transformative forces and spirit move as we were aligning with God's will.

9.  and inevitable changes in our lives, thoughts, words, and deeds; doing our best to reflect Him. We resisted the spirit of complaining, criticizing, worrying, and whining. We began to learn to reflect His goodness by exercizing His grace to one another. These transformative attitudes began to show through our expressions of language and speech and allowing change as we adjusted to new circumstances of life. Remember the cliché: "God in, God out.....?"

10. We learnt that anything can happen to anyone, any time, any where whether you are good or bad and whether you are right or wrong; no one knows what the next moment brings just as the Holy Bible says in the Book of PROVERBS 27:1 which says: "Do not boast about tomorrow, for you do not know what a day may bring forth."

11. So, it is wise to be ready and prepared for anything, any time, any where. For this world is not our home, we are just pilgrims passing through. We can die at any time or even the end of the world can happen at any time. There is no guarantee for peace, security, and safety. We walk by faith and not by sight as it is written in the Book of 2 CORINTHIANS 5:7 which says: "We live by faith, not by sight." And 1THESSALONIANS 5:3 says about the day of the LORD and any other day: "While people are saying, "Peace and safety," destruction will come on them suddenly,

as labor pains on a pregnant woman, and they will not escape."

12. We learnt that God protects, rescues, defends, and delivers whoever he chooses. He is full of mercy, compassion, grace and love for all His children. I urge you to believe in Him because the benefits cannot be numbered.

13. And finally, we learnt that God still performs miracles as He did in the days of old. HEBREWS 13:8 says:" Jesus Christ is the same yesterday and today and forever." My wife and I are a living testimony and proof of what He can do. Just believe in Him and have faith. What he did for us he can also do for you.

## SYNOPSES OF SOME DIVINE ENCOUNTERS:

According to Bible accounts:

1. ENOCK: was raptured alive to heaven as it is written in HEBREWS11:5 and the account reads as follows: "By faith Enock was taken from this life, so that he did not experience death; he could not be found, because God had taken him away. For before he was taken he was commended as one who pleased God."

2. ELIJAH: was carried away by a chariot of fire as it is recorded in 2 KINGS2:11 and the account reads: "As they were walking along and talking together, suddenly a chariot of fire and horses of fire appeared and separated the two of them, and Elijah went up to heaven in a whirlwind. Elisha saw this and cried out, "My father! My father!The chariots and horsemen of Israel!" And Elisha saw him no more."

3. MOSES: At the burning bush at Horeb, the mountain of God, as it is recorded and reported in EXODUS 3:2 and ACTS 7:30-46 "There the angel of the LORD appeared to him in flames of fire from within a bush. Moses saw that though the bush was on fire it did not burn up. When the LORD saw that he had gone to look, God called him from within the bush, "Moses! Moses! And Moses said,

"Here I am." Do not come any closer," God said, "Take off your sandals, for the place where you are standing is holy ground."

4.  SAUL/PAUL: was blinded by a bright light from heaven on his way to Damascus enroute to go and persecute the followers of Christ- Christians. As it is recorded and reported in ACTS 9:3 "As he neared Damascus on his journey, suddenly a light from heaven flashed around him. He fell to the ground and heard a voice say to him,
"Saul, Saul, why do you persecute me?"
"Who are you Lord?" Saul asked.
"I am Jesus whom you are persecuting," he replied. "Now get up and go into the city and you will be told what you must do."

5.  STEPHEN: He saw Jesus standing in heaven at his execution when he was being killed by stoning. ACTS 7:54 which says: "When they heard this they were furious and gnashed their teeth at him, but Stephen full of the Holy Spirit, looked up to heaven and saw the glory of God, and Jesus standing at the right hand of God. "Look," he said, "I see heaven open and the son of man standing at the right hand of of God."
"At this they covered their ears and, yelling at the top of their voices, they all rushed at him, dragged him out of the city and began to stone him. Meanwhile, the witnesses laid their clothes at the feet of a young man named Saul. While they were stoning him, Stephen prayed, Lord Jesus, receive my spirit. Then he fell on his knees and cried out, "Lord, do not hold this sin against them. When he had said this, he fell asleep. And Saul was there giving approval to his death."

## SUMMARY
### Written by an unknown source:

"When God puts you in the ground,
He doesn't bury you, but plants you.
When God puts you in the fire,
He doesn't burn you, but refines you.
When God puts you in the water,
He doesn't drown you, but cleanses you,
Joseph found himself in a pit, but God was planting him to be a Prime Minister in Egypt.
The three Hebrew boys- Shadreck, Misheck, and Abedenigo found themselves in a furnance of fire, but God was refining them to be governors.
Naaman found himself in water, but God was cleansing him to be a complete leader. Wherever you are and whatever happens to you, it is not by accident, but by intention and by the grace, and miracle of God. God has already designed, preordained and predestined your life. In whatever situation, circumstance, or state you find yourself in, just know that it's part of God's plan designed for you. Don't give up the good fight of faith. God cares for you and loves you. Take heart dear sons and daughters of God, you are still champions and belong to the winning team. just remember what the word of God says. PSALM 30:5 KJV- says these comforting words: "Weeping may endure for a night, but joy cometh in the morning.

This tells us that our troubles are temporay and not permanent. They will last only for a while. We should be sure that the seasons of sorrow will come and go and joy will come after we have endured some time of suffering and pain. ECCLESIASTES 3:1-8 says it much better when it says: "There is a time for everything, and season for every activity under heaven:

A time to be born and a time to die,
A time to plant and a time to uproot,
A time to tear down and a time to build,
A time to weep and a time to laugh,

A time to mourn and a time to dance,
A time to scatter stones and a time to gather them,
A time to embrace and a time to refrain,
A time to search and time to give up,
A time to keep and a time to throw away,
A time to tear and a time to mend,
A time to be silent and a time to speak,
A time to love and time to hate,
A time for war and a time for peace."

PSALM 105:1 NIV says: "Give thanks to the LORD, proclaim his name; make known to the nations what he has done."

# CHAPTER NINE

## THE GEMS AND NUGGETS THAT WERE BORN OUT OF OUR TRAGIC EXPERIENCE-THE CAR ACCIDENT

After everything was said and done, Papa Florian Joshua Kamanda, the senior Pastor and visionary of the Restoration International Christian Center, officially declared our car accident experience a miracle to the church. He intended for us to have an opportunity to share our unique testimony to the church as a way of giving glory to God; and also as a way to encourage someone that God still performs signs, wonders and miracles even in this day and age.

He had intended to hold an interview like setting in the church instead of preaching. When this did not happen, he decided that I preach instead. The date for the preaching was set for the 8th of November, 2015.

I'd already gone through so much and really was not thrilled or looking forward to preaching; because I know that preaching is a deeply spiritual activity that requires a lot of strength. It needed God's hand and the leading and touch of the Holy Spirit to be in total control in order for me to ably convey the experience and deliver the message to the church. In view of this, the only thing I had to do was to yield, submit, and surrender and let the Holy Spirit have His way.

I began to make the necessary preparations and arrangements. This needed work to listen to the Holy spirit with a spiritual ear and write down what I heard Him say to me so that I could let Him communicate His message through me as he desired and only make me His mouthpiece. Because of this I have decided to include the sermon layout and share it with the hope that it will help and touch someone as I share some spiritual insights.

THE SERMON
TITLE: GRACE WORKS:

AN EXTRACT FROM THE HIGHLIGHTS OF THE ACCIDENT STORY-SYNOPSIS OF THE CORE: SERMON-PARAPHRASED-STORY RETOLD

Greetings to all of you my brothers and sisters!
Greetings to all of you children of God!
I am grateful for the rare privilege today, to be afforded an opportunity and platform, which I take as hallowed sacred ground. I do not take this honor for granted or lightly. I am so grateful and I pray that my spirit and whole being surrenders to God so that He can use me as a vessel of clay to be His mouthpiece to correctly communicate His word. So that I may deliver His message to the hearing of His people and inspire their hearts to receive His sacred word.

You have already heard the full details of the tragic story of the car accident I shared and sang the song-the words of the song "Blessed Assurance" with me. Ironically, this whole terrible experience turned out to be a blessing in disguise; because the experience born out of this tragedy was not only divine and spiritually enriching, but priceless. There is no price tag that can be put to its value.

This does not mean that it was easy or enjoyable to go through what we went through; but it was extremely wonderful, and could not probably be experienced or earned by any other way in order for it to become a Divine Encounter. To receive a touch from the divine! To have a foretaste of glory divine, to be an heir of salvation and purchased of God, and born of His spirirt and washed in His blood.

Every person alive and living today has a story to tell born out of their life experiences. Mine, is not the only story. It's neither the first nor the last story of this nature. There are many more untold stories that are of spiritual or divine nature. My only question to you is: What is your story? Remember that your story becomes your testimony, and your testimony becomes your message that should reach, touch, edify, lift, and encourage someone that our God is alive; and indeed, that Jesus Christ is alive!

When we encounter hard times, troubles, suffering, tests, trials and tribulations, we ask ourselves questions like: "Why is life so unfair and cruel at times?" My word of encouragement I need to share with you is found in the scriptures of the Book of 2 CORINTHIANS 4:8 (NIV) which says:

"We are hard pressed on every side, but not crushed, perplexed, but not in despair, persecuted, but not abandoned, struck down, but not destroyed."

My story, experience, and tragedy is real and evidence of the meaning of this scripture. The strong hand of God rescued us! We survived the deadly blow of death the car accident nearly dealt us. We cheated death by God's grace because His grace works.

The Holy Bible has several stories of many individuals who went through untold suffering beyong human bearing. Some Bible story examples are the likes of the story of Job, Joseph, David, and Jesus Christ, to mention but a few.

JOB: The story of Job's ordeal starts with God bragging and boasting about how Job was a righteous and upright man. God was boasting about Job to Satan, the devil. Who, in turn, asked for permission, authority and power from God to persecute him. His request was granted. Consequently, Job suffered a series of tragedies. Job suffered greatly under the tormenting hand of Satan just because God had boasted about him and allowed his faith, uprightness and steadfastness to be tested through a hurricane of attacks of many forms of troubles that caused Job great suffering and grief of the greatest magnitude, levels and degrees.

Firstly, all his sons and daughters perished under the force of a great storm. Secondly, his livestock was utterly wiped out. All his animals that included herds of carmels and cattle were taken away by a band of rustlers, robbers, and thieves who killed all his herdsmen but left only one in each case so that they could go and report to Job.

Job was bombarded by report after report of tragedy after tragedy and calamity after calamity that befell him all at once. All his wealth, riches and substance just disappeared and was gone like a puff of smoke.

The lesson we must learn through this story of Job's tragedies is that: we might be going through trials and tribulations just because God is boasting about you and me and has allowed our faith to be tested. Even Abraham was asked to offer his only son Isaac as a sacrifice of worship to God. But God has always come through because His grace works. God's grace works.

The cause of your sufferings, troubles, trials and tribulations may be that God is bragging about you. Surley, if you are in good standing with God, He will boast about you. Job was hard pressed from all sides, bombarded by terrible misfortunes that took away all his fortunes and blessings, but God's grace worked because he was not crushed, perplexed, even though he was in despair. He was persecuted but not abandoned, struck down but not destroyed, because grace worked. God's grace works!

Look at what followed: restoration of all that he had lost. It was doubled, tripled and quadrupled:
Restoration of all his children
Retoration of all his animals

Restoration of his wealth and health
The restoration of Job's fame and fortune coupled with peace. He led a life of jubilation, celebration, and restitution because grace works.

I encourage you all my brothers and sisters to be strong, firm and trust in the LORD for he is faithful. God's divine providence remains a mystery to all of us.

JOSEPH: Look at the life and fate of Joseph. Just because of his dreams and visions Joseph suffered hatred, redicule, jealousy and imprisonment despite his innocence. Joseph had a divine calling upon his life. God's hand and blessings were upon him, but did he walk an easy road to the fulfillment of his destiny? The answer is No! it was a tough and rough road to travel for him to finally ascend to the position of promotion.

Do observe also that Jacob, Joseph's father, despite being the authority figure and Joseph's role model, at one time questioned his own son's sanity. Jacob significantly doubted his son's soundness of mind and actually told him he had lost it because he'd dreamt that his parents and siblings would one day bow down before him.

.As if that was not enough Joseph's siblings were possessed by a Spirit of Jealousy because of the favor upon his life from God and his biological father Jacob so much so that his brothers plotted to kill him and ended up selling him into slavery to the Ishmaelites.

The gems or nuggets in Joseph's life story and experiences are that:

You and I might be suffering many trials and tribulations because of God's favor upon our lives. This could be because of our divine calling, visions, and dreams or even talents and gifts endowed upon you and me. These might cause others to persecute you because of jealousy and try to dissuade you, discourage you and try to deter you from reaching your divine purpose, goal, and destiny which God gave you as the purpose of your life.

So why should you and I wonder why and keep asking where the suffering is coming from and perceive ourselves as innocent victims. We should not play victim and wallow in self pity. Joseph did not do any of that. Joseph's brothers teased him, mocked him, criticized and insulted him. They laughed at him and called him the dreamer. This was intended to discourage him. It was an attempt to stop him from believing in his God given visions and dreams. They went further to even try and kill him and his dreams.

Reflect and look back at your own life and ask yourself some questions. My question to you is: What have you gone through? May be you have gone through some of these experiences. Like Joseph, may be God has made you a coat of many colors-denoting many gifts, talents, abilities, blessings and favor upon your life which are attracting and causing other people to be jealousy of you; which results in them mistreating and abusing you or even planning to kill you. May be there have been attempts on your life; your friends or even family trying to kill and eliminate you. Just remember that God's grace works!

Remember how Joseph was even thrown in a pit. Some people will even try to bury you in a pit of oblivion so that you are completely forgotten. See how Reuben, Jacob's eldest son, who was Joseph's brother, had secretly and quietly come up with a plan to rescue Joseph. He was working on a personal rescue plan. God might not need a "Reuben" kind of help because God's grace works and His hand is not too short to rescue his own that He has chosen. Grace works!

Even if Joseph was sold into slavery to the Ishmaelites and bought by Pharoah's Army commnder Portipher, nothing changed the trajectory of the fulfillment of his destiny. Even though Portipher's wife coveted Joseph and attempted to rape him, and falsely accused him and had him thrown in jail, God's hand and plan never changed. After escaping from Portipher's adulterous wife's grabby hands, God's favor never left Joseph despite being in a prison cell where he still found favor.

While in jail Joseph became a leader there and interpreted dreams of Pharoah's Cup-bearer and baker. both dream interpretations were proved accurate and both became true. Indeed, the grand finale came when Joseph stood before King Pharoah and interpreted his dreams with accuracy and gave Pharoah a strategy to grow and store food and save his people. Yet again, this is the mystery of God's providence, Joseph was appointed Prime Minister at once despite all the odds against him.

His enemies, tormentors, and accusers became his subordinates in a wink of an eye. Portipher, his wife, all the prison warders, and all the people of Egypt became his subjects and all fell under his authority, power, and rule. Just look at how amazing God's power is that would suddenly bring Portipher, Pharoah's Army Commander immediately come under Joseph's authority and power. And was assigned by Pharaoh to make sure Joseph had the security needed around him as it befits the appointed Prime Minister who at this point, became second in the chain of command. Just look at what followed:

Restoration of his childhood visions
Restoration and fulfillment of his dreams
Restoration of His destiny despite obscurity
Restoration of his innonce against all false accusations
Restoration of his preordained purpose, predestined authority, dreams, divine calling, and ultimate fulfillment of God's plan of his life. God's grace worked. Grace works. God's grace is at work and in action in our lives now and forever. It is written that our God is the same yesterday, today, and forever.

DAVID: David's life story is not only unique but unusual. After King Saul had disobeyed God and had fallen from grace. King Saul's disobedience is where this old saying, "Obedience is better than sacrifice" originates. This old saying was born out of Saul's disobedience when he decided to keep some fat livestock after

God had instructed him not to keep anything after defeating the enemy he had given him the victory.

The Prophet Samuel told Saul that God had rejected him as King of Israel. God then instructed the Prophet Samuel to go and anoint a new King from Jesse's house whom God called: "A man after my (God's} own heart." God was not looking for physical looks or good appearances of the likes of Eliab, Shamma, Abinadab, and all the other sons in the house of Jesse. God had chosen the young David on whom the anointing oil poured out when he was called from the pasture land where he was tending the family livestock.

This is ironic, because the shepherd boy, David, became the "shepherd" of the nation of Israel. David had killed the bears and lions to protect his father's animals and ultimately the enemies of the nation of Israel. This trail of threats and victories scored by David all started in the pasture lands against the wolves and then went to Goliath the giant who posed a prolonged threat and struck feared in the hearts of all; that included the King Saul and his generals and all the armies of Israel who, presumably had experience in warfare.

This is ironic because David killed the bears and lions that came after his flock while he was in the pasture lands. David himself actually likened Goliath to those wolves he had killed when he faced off the giant in the valley of Ellah. In apparent shock to all, David killed the giant Goliath in the same way he had killed the wild animals that had threaned and come after his flock.

What this indirectly tells us is: whatever giants may stand in our own lives, God has empowered us to defeat, kill and eliminate the giants, and emerge conqurors because God's grace works. This is ironic indeed because David himself wrote in the famous and widely quoted psalm, Psalm 23 that says: "Though I walk through the valley of death, I will fear no evil for you are with me." God was with David when he walked through the shadow of the valley of death in the real physical valley of Ellah which supposedly was to be his valley of death but David feared no evil because God's grace was with him.

Despite using the most primitive and unsophisticated weapon after rejecting King Saul's armor. In spite of this seeming disadvantage, David prevailed over Goliath and the Philistines. God, and only God deserved the glory, which He alone is worthy, not sophisticated weapons or skill, ability, experience, physical prowess and might. It is not about any man's valor or ability but the grace of God. Grace works!

Despite his innocence, King Saul continued hunting down David like a wild animal and rendered him a fugitive, and a criminal who had committed no crime, in spite of all this, David still became King over Israel.

Ask yourself some personal questions: "Who is the Saul persuing you? "Who is the the Goliath intimidating or threatening to destroy you and God's purpose for your life?" Just have faith and believe that your destiny is safe in God's hands because His grace is sufficient for you just as the Apostle Paul wrote in one of his epistles.

In other instances, you are counted out and not even considered for Kingship like David. He was almost disqualified, but God qualified him and He can qualify you as well because God qualifies the unqualified and disqualifies the qualified by men's standards. Somebody said: "God does not call the equipped, but equips the called." God can do this through the most unlikely ways. Indeed, God works in mysterious ways as the Bible says.

Sometimes God can use afflictions, suffering, troubles, problems and even trials and tribulations of many forms to take you to your destiny. No one can comprehend the ways of God. For who can give Him counsel on what or how He decides to do anything. Just look at my story and many others and tell me if such calamities and tragedies would cause anyone to worship or even to praise

God. Look at the afflictions of Job, Joseph, David, Stephen and many more, and also look at your own life.

God is no respecter of persons as the Bible says. He does whatever He chooses to whoever He uses for His own purposes and glory. He is a good and holy God who intends no evil and does not co-habit with sin, iniquity, transgression or any other form of unrighteousness. He is a perfect and loving Father to all His children and creation. His grace is free to all who are willing to receive it. It is readily accessible to all.

Prophetically, God prepared a table for David in the presence of his enemies like Saul, his own brothers who despised and discouraged him from fighting Goliath. David went through many trials and tribulations.

He went through a lot of troubles, sufferings, and challenges from the day of his anointing, and even before, up to the day he ascended to the throne to become King of Israel. David was God's choice of the second King of Israel who became the most significant King in the entire history of all the successive Kings of Israel after saul's fall and death. Remember that David was almost disqualified by his own father Jesse until Samuel the Prophet insisted and asked: "Don't you have another son? Are these the only sons you have?" David was almost ignored and left out.

There's one more little boy taking care of the sheep." Jesse answered, and alas! This was God's choice-David.

In retrospect after David slew Goliath, Saul was possessed by an evil Spirit due to the passion of jealousy after he heard the women sin songs of praises for David saying: "A thousand for King Saul and ten thousand for for David. David's fame and heroism afflicted Saul. Consequently, the rulers of Israel had the task of choosing the best Musician to exorcise and appease the demon that had possessed saul. David was chosen and became the royal Musician at Saul's palace. King Saul, in his frenzy of demonic jealousy threw spears in an attempt to kill David and thwart God's plan for David.

Ironically, Jonathan, Saul's son and heir apparent became the spy and informer of David and kept him safe from harm and the murderous intentions of Saul. God's favor and grace was upon David. This teaches us that all sorts of bad things can happen to you and me, but God's plans cannot be thwarted, hindered, blocked, or stopped by anything or anyone. Ask yourself this question: "Who is the Saul in your life who is trying to destroy or stop God's plans for your destiny?" Victory is certain because God's grace works and His hand is upon you and me.

Despite all this, David did not harbor anger, rancor, revenge, bitterness, resentment or any form of unforgiveness against Saul or any of his enemies. Observe that even when Saul was made available for him to kill him both in the cave and when he found him deep in sleep he did not take revenge. David did not do any harm either to Saul, his army or Generals who were pursuing him. David showed grace and a clean heart by just cutting a piece of saul's royal regalia and took his spear in one and the other event both in the cave and when he found him in deep slumber in spite of David's men urging him to kill Saul. David refused and said he could not touch or lay hands on the anointed of God.

In spite of the Philistines King and his generals knowing that David had killed Goliath their war hero, they still made peace with him during his troubled times as he was running away from Saul. They gave him his own piece of land at Ziglag. God can cause your enemies to be at peace with you just as the Bible says.

Even when the Philistine commanders advised their King to send David back and not allow him to be their ally against Israel. Upon his return to Ziglag, his capital, David found Ziglag routed, ransacked, and totally destroyed. When they saw this, David's men conspired to revolt and kill him, but David encouraged himself in the Lord and enquired of the Lord if he should pursue his enemies.

God allowed him to go after his enemies and when he found them he fought and defeated them and took back all that they had stolen from Ziglag. He recovered everything that they had stolen.

This teaches us that before we make any important decision we should ask God. It also teaches us not to put our faith in men because men can let us down. Men can disappoint us but God will not leave alone or forsake us.

God is our defender! Always encourage and strengthen yourself in the Lord and He will never leave you alone. What followed after the conquest of Ziglag?
Total Restoration of both women and children
Total restoration of all the substance that had been stolen by the Amalekites from David and his people. Also David did something remarkable by deciding to share with all his men including those who had refused to go to war after the enemies, the Amalekites thieves and robbers with him who had destroyed Ziglag.
Restoration also came even after his own son Absalom had led a rebellion against him. The revolt was foiled and all his enemies killed in the war of that coup de tat.

David was constantly restored even after he had committed a grieveous sin of plotting after and killing his loyal soldier Uriah whose wife he had committed adultery with. David was not a perfect man. He messed up many times but repented and God was always faithful to forgive him though other negative consequences followed like the death of His son with Bathsheba whom Uriah's wife had given birth to. David's sins also caused the eventual division of the Kingdom of Israel. But nevertheless, David is still known as a man after God's own heart and a legendary warrior boy who slew Goliath and the greatest King of Israel.

Finally, Jesus Christ, the son of God and our Messiah's crucifixion, death and resurrection shows us human suffering beyond comprehension that surpasses all other forms of human suffering. even though Jesus Christ knew his betrayer, he still ate at the same table with him-Judas Iscariot because of his grace and love which goes beyond our human understanding.

When we look back at the events in the garden of Getseman when Jesus was being arrested and taken away by the ceasar's soldiers;Despite Marcus being his persecutor and tormentor having his ear chopped off by Simon Peter in his rage and violent feat, trying to wage war against Jesus' captors Jesus Christ still picked up his chopped ear, healed him and restored him. Grace worked. Have you ever had your own Gethsemane crisis where God's will must prevail? Or your own will conflicts with God's?

In spite of Simon Peter denying Christ, upon His resurrection, Jesus never reminded Peter of his misdeeds and denial. Christ never blamed, accused, judged or convicted him of all the bad things he did and was outrightly guilty of had Jesus come to judge and condemn the wrongdoers. Jesus never focused on the wrongs of humanity but on grace, mercy and forgiveness of all sins of humanity because Jesus Christ himself is grace and love.

While Jesus was hanging on the cross, He still said: "father, forgive them for they know not what they do!" This is the grand finale, the culmination and total embodiment of the fullness of grace, truth, and love demonstrated by God himself hanging on the cross for our sins. Despite the Father's anger, and near intention of almost destroying those torturing His own son. Jesus did not negatively confront any of His enemies after His resuerrection except the defeated foe, the devil, Satan himself whom he defeated on the cross for us and on our behalf. Grace worked and grace won and will always win over the works of the enemy.

Grace worked, grace works, and grace will and is still working and will work forevermore!
There is mercy in grace!
There is love in grace!
There is truth in grace!
There is compassion in grace!
There is forgiveness in grace!
There is restoration in grace!
There is reconciliation in grace!
There is restitution in grace!
There is reparation in grace!
There is repentance in grace!

There is atonement in grace!
There is propitiation in grace!

Grace works! Grace is working and will always work at all times! Do not worry, fear, or complain when you find yourself in a pit like Joseph, God is not burying you, but planting you into the ground to grow you to fruitfulness, greatness, and the fulfillment of your destiny, calling, vision, dream, and divine purpose. He has given you authority and power and rulership over the power of the enemy.

When you find yourself in deep waters of life, God is washing you like Naaman to great positions, and status of leadership.
When you find yourself in hot fires of life, like Shadreck, Misheck, and Abegonigo, just know that God is refining you for you to have dominion and govern like the three Hebrew boys.

When you find yourself in a den of hungry Lions like Daniel, God is exonerating you, declaring you innocent, and confirming you to be on top of the rungs of the ladder of leadership for His own glory!
All glory be to God! Praise God and worship His holy name!

In closing, all the Bible story individuals used as examples were hard pressed on every side, but not crushed, perplexed, but not in despair, persecuted, but not abandoned, struck down, but not destroyed.
Therefore, be encouraged and strengthened my brothers and sisters as it is written in 2 CORINTHIANS 4:8

JAMES 1:1 also reiterates these words and says:

"Consider it pure joy, my brothers, whenever you face trials of many kinds, because you know that the testing of your faith develops perseverance, perseverance must finish its work so that you may be mature and complete, not lacking anything. If any of you lacks wisdom, he should ask God, who gives generously to all without finding fault, and it will be given to him. But when he asks, he must believe and not doubt, because he who doubts is like the wave of the sea, blown and tossed by the wind. The man should not think that he will receive anything from the Lord; he is a double minded man, unstable in all he does."

ROMANS8:38 says:
"Not only so, we also rejoice in our sufferings, because we know that suffering produces perseverance, perseverance, character, and character hope, and hope does not disappoint us, because God has poured out his love by the Holy Spirit whom He has given us. You see, just at the right time, when we were powerless, Christ died for us the ungodly."

ROMANS 8:35 says:
"Who shall separate us from the love of Christ?

Shall trouble or hardship or persecution or famine or nakedness or danger or sword? As it is written;
For your sake we face death all the day long;
We are considered as sheep to be slaughtered.
No, in all things we are more than conquerors through him who loved us. For I am convinced that neither death nor life, neither angels nor demons, neither the present nor the future, nor any powers, neither height nor depth, nor anything else in all creation, will be able to separate us from the love of God that is in Jesus Christ Jesus, our LORD."

This is the critical question you and I must ask ourselves as we reflect on the stories of our own lives in times of retrospection, self-examination, self-evaluation, and self-introspection.


END

By the grace of God, after all that we went through, On the 12th of March, my wife and I renewed our vows on our 12th marriage Anniversary in Indiana, Indianapolis USA at Restoration International Christian Center. This was a wonderful time of celebration and jubilation! Celebrating life and our marriage and family. God is good. Instead of a funeral ceremony we were celebrating our second wedding ceremony after the first one that took place in Africa-Zambia-Lusaka at Mulungushi International Conference Center onth 13th of march, 2004. Our children celebrated this second wedding with us: Our first born child, our son Rungano who is now eleven years old, followed by our daughter, Rutendo, who is eight, and Rudo who is two. We give glory to God!

# ABOUT AUTHOR

A multi talented artiste at the core, an educator in the field of Expressive Arts. A Music and English teacher and taught at Solwezi Teacher's College in Africa-Zambia in the Northwestern province. A trainer of Music and has travelled widely in the USA training Praise and Worship groups. A recording Artiste and also called " The Teacher," and trained in Christian Arts in Bloemfontein, Orange Freestate in South Africa from 1996 to 2001. Pioneer in planting schools in the Arts in general and trained at Evelyn Hone College of Arts in Zambia- Lusaka-1987-1989. Holds a degree in General Studies from IUPUI- USA-Indiana University. Pioneer in Educational reforms and co-authored National Educational materials in the study area of Expressive Arts in Zambia. A Community and National leader at various levels-served as PAC Chairman of NWP with the Zambia National Arts Council and National vice president of the Zambia Association of Musicians and Conflict Resolutions Mediator and facilitator. Educator, life coach and preacher. A leader with diverse gifts and talents serving as Ministry and Music Director with RICC Pastoral Board in Indiana USA.

CPSIA information can be obtained at www.ICGtesting.com
Printed in the USA
BVOW02*1941190416

444801BV00001B/60/P